The Fruit and Gifts of the Holy Spirit

By Wayne E. Caldwell
Edited by Armor D. Peisker

The Wesley Press
Marion, Indiana

The Fruit and Gifts of the Holy Spirit is an Aldersgate Doctrinal Series publication. Written by Wayne E. Caldwell and edited by Armor D. Peisker, this book is one of a series of doctrinal publications designed to promote a better understanding of the holiness movement's doctrine.

The **Aldersgate Doctrinal Series** is developed cooperatively by denominations having a common theological heritage and holding membership in the Aldersgate Publications Association as follows: Churches of Christ in Christian Union, Church of the Nazarene, Congregational Methodist, Evangelical Friends Alliance, Evangelical Methodist, Free Methodist, The Missionary Church, The Wesleyan Church. Various parts of the cooperative Aldersgate products are produced by member publishing houses of APA.

The **Editorial Board** for the Aldersgate publications includes: Keith W. Drury, Dorothy Barratt, Howard B. Castle, Ronald D. Driggers, Douglas Feazell, Michael Reynolds, Richard L. Spindle, Catherine Stonehouse, Stan Toler.

International Standard Book Number: 0-89827-005-7
The Wesley Press; Marion, Indiana 46952
© 1979 by The Wesley Press. All rights reserved.
First edition published 1979
Printed in the United States of America

Contents

INTRODUCTION

"Life is not for me any longer a tangle of circumstances, a series of laborious engagements . . . long stretches of plodding in comparative darkness . . . There is a new quiet of heart, a new restfulness of soul, a new quickness of consent to all that I think to be the will of God."

This is the way one man describes how things changed for him with the coming of the Holy Spirit. He was brought to that happy condition, he says, as he searched the Scriptures to find a reason for the dissatisfaction and restlessness deep within himself.

This points up how it is that the Scriptures instruct and lead us into the way of truth. If we would rightly understand the Holy Spirit and His work in the lives of persons today, we must go to the Bible. The Bible, not human experience, is the final authority.

A reason so many of the present-day cults attract youth is that they emphasize feeling and experience more than doctrine — the mystical rather than the rational. Contemporary human experience is important as it may illustrate and demonstrate Bible teaching; but the Bible sounds the standard pitch to which all human experience must be tuned.

Our purpose in this book is to listen for the Bible's tone — to hear especially what it says about the fruit and gifts of the Holy Spirit. We are particularly interested to know how they are related and what may be their distinctions.

Thus our focus will be the Bible — not what this or that person experienced. We will look into the Word of God and find out for ourselves what this book has to say about the Holy Spirit — His fruit and His gifts. What matters most is not what someone has felt inside them. What matters to us is what the Bible says.

CHRISTIANS BEAR FRUIT

Relevant Scriptures: John 15:1-10, 16; 1 Corinthians 13:1-13; 2 Corinthians 9:8-11.

"Salvation," someone has well said, "is not connected only with the stopping of evil. To that must be added the practice of good."

This highlights the fact that continuing to walk a consistent Christian life every day in the power of the Holy Spirit is as important as experiencing initially God's forgiveness; as important as experiencing the infilling with His Spirit.

Justification and entire sanctification are, indeed, essential crises; but they relate to life as definitely as does natural birth. It is, in fact, a mistake to stress a crisis apart from the process of living.

There is nothing clearer in Scripture than the relation of the Holy Spirit to the daily life of the believer. The Spirit's action and work covers all of life from first to last.

The Holy Spirit comes to the life of every

believer at the point of repentance and personal acceptance of Christ as Saviour. The Holy Spirit gives new life, even eternal life, in regeneration or conversion[1]; He is the Spirit of sonship making possible our adoption as children of God[2]; He is the Spirit of holiness that we may be entirely sanctified[3]; He is the Spirit of glory transforming and changing us into His own spiritual likeness[4]; and He is the Spirit of promise assuring us of our resurrection, our ultimate triumph over death[5].

At the moment of the New Birth the leadership of the Holy Spirit is available[6]. The new believer immediately has the potential to be completely controlled by the Spirit as he yields his life[7]. Growth is the natural outcome as faith is increased[8]; as the Word of God is studied[9]; as prayer and communion with God through His Son is engaged in[10]; and as the self is yielded to the leadership of the Holy Spirit[11].

The primary purpose of the Holy Spirit is to clarify and apply the revelation of God as given in and by Jesus Christ. It is not the Holy Spirit's basic work to produce spectacular manifestations. He is the Spirit of Christ[12]. Jesus said, "When He, the Spirit of truth, comes, . . . He shall glorify Me; for He shall take of Mine, and shall disclose it to you" (John 16:13-14, NASB).

[1]See end of each chapter for these related Bible references.

4

When a person is born again, he is prepared for a life in the will of God. With a new nature and the life of Christ in him, the believer has a vital relationship with God and to other believers. He also has the Holy Spirit in his mind and consciousness.

All these things set the stage for an effective expression of a moral life in keeping with the character of God. Even a young believer, with all of his immaturity, has a definite change in his life and can achieve a high moral balance because he can know and experience the will of God by the help of the Spirit.

Spiritual maturity, however, is achieved only as the new believer experiences growth. That takes time.

The degree to which the Holy Spirit fills, controls, and directs the new believer will determine the extent to which growth and development occur. The Spirit's ministry includes that of teaching, guiding, assuring, inspiring worship, and guiding prayer. All of these things affect the quality of the believer's life as it reflects the holiness of God.

The ministry of the Spirit of God also works in the inner life of the believer, producing in him the fruit of the Spirit. The first five chapters of this book consider various aspects of the fruit borne by the Spirit in a believer's life.

These three general observations are listed for the sake of clarity and direction:

5

1. The fruit of the Spirit is demonstrated to some degree in the life of every Christian. It is not the primary, or even the secondary, purpose of this study to distinguish between that fruit which is borne by a newborn babe in Christ and a more mature believer with years of experience.

2. It is noteworthy that "fruit of the Spirit" is not plural in form but singular. This indicates that each element is needed to make up the complete unit, like the separate petals of a flower or the single grape of a cluster. The use of the singular "fruit" further indicates that the various aspects refer to character rather than to conduct. It is something related to being rather than doing.

3. The fruit of the Spirit is produced in relationship with other persons. The believer must maintain an integral relationship with God through the Holy Spirit, but the fruit is borne in association with other people. Fruitbearing cannot be a solo operation.

THE NATURE OF THE FRUIT OF THE SPIRIT

The term "fruit of the Spirit" describes the results in a believer's life as the Holy Spirit is allowed to control and "breathe through" that life. A person so-controlled reenacts the very life that was in Christ as explained in 1 Corinthians 13.

In the opening verses of that passage, the Apostle Paul compares love with the ability to speak in different languages, to preach or to prophesy, and with mysteries, with knowledge, and with the faith that works miracles. All of these abilities are discounted as inferior to love.

Love abides and stands supreme. It is superior to all other virtues, abilities, or graces. It is the fruit of the Spirit. Benevolences, sufferings, pain, death, even a willing martyrdom are meaningless if devoid of love.

The traits and character of love, the greatest of all evidences of life in the Spirit as described and depicted in 1 Corinthians 13:4-7, are in direct contrast to what was true in the Corinthian church. The Corinthians were impatient, discontented, envious, inflated, selfish, suspicious, resentful, censorious, and unmindful of the feelings or interests of others. In general, they were lacking the fruit of the Spirit in their lives.

The fruit of the Spirit is the spiritual harvest produced within the life of the believer by the Holy Spirit. As has been noted, fruit is a collective noun in singular form which suggests the many-sided yet interrelated qualities of the life of Christ which are produced within the personality of the believer and manifested in a Christlike walk. *This fruit is not a human "work" which results from individual effort or a personal self-discipline.* Man works, but God gives the fruit.

The Spirit's fruit is God's nature in Christ reproduced in the believer. The Holy Spirit produces this fruit by imparting God's holiness which is manifested as Christlikeness of character.

It should also be noted that there are various terms in Scripture used to describe the fruit of the Spirit. In John 15:1-8, it is evident that by "abiding in the vine," by being "cleansed by the Word," and by being "pruned by the Gardener," one will bear fruit, much fruit, and more fruit. For as the believer abides in Christ, the life of Christ will, by the Holy Spirit, produce the character and fruit of Christ, who is the Vine, in the believer who is the branch.

Again, when a believer refuses to let sin dwell in his mortal body after being made alive from trespasses and sins, fruit unto holiness will be borne[13].

When we look at the context of Galatians 5:22-23 (the fruit of the Spirit passage), it becomes clear that this fruit is the result of living life daily in the strength of the Holy Spirit, having the flesh crucified and then doing those things which nurture spiritual life[14].

Although God is the source of all the fine qualities which constitute the fruit of the Spirit in the Christlike life, we too have certain responsibilities to make a diligent effort to grow and develop in all the aspects of spiritual maturity[15]. These aspects of fruit can be experienced in increasing measure. The Apostle Peter assures us, "If these things be in you and abound, they make you so that ye shall be neither barren nor unfruitful in the knowledge of our Lord Jesus Christ" (2 Peter 1:8).

The Corinthians, like the Galatian people, developed a neat little formula of the Christian life. They thought that by pleasing God, in doing His will and being faithful to all that He said, they would be holy and He would bless them. But it didn't work out that way for them any more than it works out that way today.

The error is to think that Christian character is produced by habitual obedience to rules and regulations, or by participation in ceremonies of the church calendar. But Paul, like others before and after him, taught that holiness is something that God plants in the believer. It is a seed and a life in the Spirit which develops and blossoms in spite of all hindrances.

Even in the Old Testament this was understood. Psalm 1 is a great example of this principle. The believer who takes time to meditate on God's Word will be like a tree planted by streams of water. The tree produces fruit at the proper time, and its leaf does not wither.

This is in stark contrast to the wicked and the unbeliever. The character of the ungodly is like chaff. There is not a hint that the tree could bring forth anything but fruit or that the ungodly would ever be anything but chaff.

Jeremiah enlarges upon the psalmist's description when he writes,

> "This is what the Lord says: 'Cursed is the one who trusts in man, who depends on flesh for his strength and whose heart turns away from the Lord. He will be like a bush in the wastelands; he will not see prosperity when it comes. He will dwell in the parched places of the desert, in a salt land where no one lives. But blessed is the man who trusts in the Lord, whose confidence is in him. He will be like a tree planted by the water that sends out its roots by the stream. It does not fear when heat comes; its leaves are always green. It has no worries in a year of drought and never fails to bear fruit' " (Jeremiah 17:5-8, NIV).

The psalmist and Jeremiah agree on the necessity and inevitability of fruit for the righteous. The man who trusts the Lord *will* bear fruit. Isaiah 5 and Psalm 92 are two further examples in the Old Testament of this principle of fruitfulness, with various figures of speech being used to express the truth.

John the Baptist, as the forerunner of Jesus, had done his homework and was filled with the Spirit when he said, "Bring forth fruit in keeping with your repentance, . . . the axe is already laid at the root of the trees; every tree therefore that does not bear fruit is cut down and thrown into the fire" (Matthew 3:8, 10, NASB).

John's teaching also paved the way for the more explicit expression of Jesus that fruit is the true clue to character because there is such a close correspondence between fruit and that which produces it. In His Sermon on the Mount Jesus warned that false prophets would try to deceive but that they, too, could be known by their fruit. This is always a safe guide because, "Every good tree bears good fruit, but a bad tree bears bad fruit. A good tree cannot bear bad fruit, and a bad tree cannot bear good fruit. Every tree that does not bear good fruit is cut down and thrown into the fire. Thus, by their fruit you will recognize them" (Matthew 7:17-20, NIV).

The Master makes the contrast even more vivid when He states, "Make a tree good and its fruit will be good, or make a tree bad and its fruit will be bad, for a tree is recognized by its fruit" (Matthew 12:33, NIV).

From the teaching of Jesus we may conclude that fruit is not something which can be superimposed by external means. The fruit must not be confused with good habits or with conformity to authority or law. Fruit is the result of the Spirit of God working directly in a believer's life and character. There is no other way to get fruit or to bear fruit. It must come from inside.

But there is a manward side that must not be overlooked. In the bearing of fruit, more fruit, and much fruit, man is not idle. Both God and man function in their spheres in harmony and union to produce the fruit. This is explicit through the use of the figures of the vine and the branches in John 15:1-10.

A vine, like a tree, has one purpose — to produce fruit. A branch also finds its true purpose when it grows on the vine and bears fruit. The farmer's purpose is to cultivate and water so that the vine bears a maximum crop.

Jesus is the true vine. The Father is the Farmer, and the believing Christian is a branch. In a mystical union between a believer and Christ there is a union by which fruit is borne and by that union alone. Abiding in the vine is not a passive thing. One must "fight the good fight of faith" (1 Timothy 6:12) and "work out your salvation" to the end. On the other hand: "It is God who works in you to will and to act according to his good purpose" (Philippians 2:12-13, NIV).

So we see that while God uses human means, Christian character and fruitfulness is not a human product. The Spirit unites persons to himself so that there is a continual flow of power and grace which produces fruit just as the sap which flows through the stem of the vine to the branch.

A person must trust in the Word, obey it, meditate on it, and delight in it. Fruit is inevitable when these conditions exist. In this God is well pleased and glorified.

CULTIVATION OF THE FRUIT

Paul's exhortation in 2 Corinthians 6:1 that

Christians are to be "workers together with Him" and his own exemplary word of personal experience show the importance of cultivation if the ground is to bear fruit. If there are dwarfed and scrubby bushes which have barely enough life to support a few leaves with no fruit brought to perfection, the fault lies at the root of the tree. Cultivation is needed. Christians may well ask themselves with searching earnestness why it is, with such possibilities offered them, so little fruit is borne.

The best conditions for the growth of the fruit of the Spirit are provided by the fellowship of believers. Without the church and such fellowship as it affords, growth and fruitage will be stunted or not at all. The fruit of the Spirit grows as we relate to others who are also bearing fruit. Growth as a Christian over a period of years will be evidenced in the quality and abundance of the fruit that is borne. This is a sure law. It cannot be successfully challenged or altered any more than we can change the natural laws of seeding, cultivation, and harvest.

SUMMARY

The crises experiences of conversion and entire sanctification are important and necessary; but they are still only the beginning steps to a fruitful Christian life. This is true because the Holy Spirit, the Spirit of Jesus, in the life of the believer affects every aspect of daily walk, manifesting His work especially in the believer's attitudes toward and relationships with other persons.

In all of these circumstances the Holy Spirit assists the believer to demonstrate the fact that love — love for God and for other persons — is the basic characteristic of the Spirit's fruit. While the Christian bears all of this good fruit because the Spirit is present and at work within him, he is responsible to so discipline himself and so nurture his spiritual life that he may constantly increase in fruitfulness and in his service in the kingdom of the Lord.

What Do You Think About These?

1. Of the Bible and human experience, which should be the final authority for understanding God's work in human lives? Why? (See Introduction.)

2. What is the primary purpose of the Holy Spirit in the world today — to produce spectacular manifestations, or to clarify and apply God's revelation in Jesus Christ?

3. Can even a newborn babe in Christ bear fruit to some degree?

4. Explain why fruit of the Spirit is in singular form (not fruits of the Spirit) in the New Testament.

5. Could a person fully bear the fruit of the Spirit if he were totally isolated from all other human beings?

6. How is the fruit of the Spirit produced — by man obeying the Bible in all things, or by God's action inside of a person?

7. What are some of the things we can to do provide an atmosphere conducive to growth and fruit bearing?

If You Want to Dig a Little Deeper

The following terms appear in this chapter. What do you understand each to mean?

forgiveness
filled with the Spirit
justification
entire sanctification
repentance

conversion
regeneration
adoption
eternal life
born again

Bible References Related to This Chapter.

[1]John 3:5, 8; Titus 3:5-6
[2]Romans 8:15; Galatians 4:6
[3]Romans 8:5
[4]2 Corinthians 3:18; 1 Peter 4:14
[5]Romans 8:11; Ephesians 1:13-14; 4:30
[6]1 Corinthians 3:16
[7]Romans 12:1-2
[8]Hebrews 11:6
[9]1 Peter 2:2

[10] 1 Thessalonians 5:17
[11] Romans 8:9
[12] 2 Corinthians 3:17
[13] Romans 6:11-13, 22
[14] Galatians 5:16, 24-25; 6:7-8
[15] 2 Peter 1:5-8

FRUIT SHOWS

Relevant Scriptures: Romans 7:4; 2 Corinthians 9:8-11; Ephesians 5:8-21; Philippians 1:9-11; Colossians 1:10-13; James 3:17-18; 2 Peter 1:1-11.

The experience of a young nurse illustrates the inner authority and outward influence of the fruitbearing Christian. She relates: "On several occasions I have had patients ask me if I am a Christian. This really made me stop and think. Then I began to inquire of the questioners why they asked or how they knew. I was informed it showed!

"I was surprised, because I had not said a word to any of the patients about religion. I was told they knew by my smile, or my actions, or by the way I talked, the way I treated them. Unawares, I had been carrying on a silent ministry."

Indeed, the Spirit's fruit shows in many and varied ways — in almost as many ways as there are individual Christians. This might be expected, for if there is one thing in the created universe more apparent than any other, it is the infinite variety which permeates the whole. It is no less true when it comes to the spiritual creativity of God within the heart and consciousness of mankind.

Not only is every person different in background, in physical and personality characteristics, but also in understanding, in ability, and in potential. This opens the way for the Spirit of God to work creatively in vastly different ways in the lives of individuals.

VARIETY IN FRUITBEARING

While each Christian may and probably does possess a measure of each quality of the Spirit's fruit, it is certain that individual believers will variously and in differing measures manifest the fruit of the Spirit.

Many varieties of Christian fruitfulness are given in the New Testament. Some of these are tabulated below in the New Testament sequence. The terms used in this tabulation are from the New International Version. No kind of fruit is repeated in the listing, although it may appear in several of the references.

In contrast, the fruit in the unbeliever's life is also listed in New Testament sequence. Here again no kind of evil fruit is listed more than once, though it may actually appear in more than one reference.

Believer

Romans 5:3-5 —
  perseverance
  character
  hope
  love

2 Corinthians 9:8-11 —
  good work
  righteousness
  generosity
  thanksgiving

Galatians 5:22 —
  joy
  peace
  patience
  kindness
  goodness
  faithfulness
  gentleness
  self-control

Ephesians 5:9 —
  truth

Colossians 1:10-11 —
  knowledge of God
  endurance

1 Timothy 6:11 —
  godliness

James 3:17 —
  purity
  peacefulness
  consideration
  submissiveness
  mercy
  impartiality
  sincerity

2 Peter 1:5-7 —
  knowledge
  brotherly kindness

Unbeliever

Matthew 15:19 —
  evil thoughts
  murder
  adultery
  sexual immorality
  thievery
  false testimony
  slander

Romans 1:29-32 —
  every kind of wickedness
  evil
  greed
  depravity
  envy
  strife
  deceit
  malice

  gossip
  hate toward God
  insolence
  arrogance
  boastfulness
  inventiveness in doing evil
  disobedience to parents
  senselessness
  faithlessness
  heartlessness
  ruthlessness

Romans 13:13 —
  orgies
  drunkenness
  debauchery
  dissension
  jealousy

1 Corinthians 5:10 —
  immorality
  trickery
  idolatry

2 Corinthians 12:20 —
  quarreling
  anger
  factions
  disorderliness

Galatians 5:19-21 —
  impurity
  witchcraft
  hate
  rage
  selfish ambition

1 Timothy 1:9-10 —
  lawlessness
  rebellion
  ungodliness
  sin
  unholiness
  irreligiousness
  patricide
  matricide
  perversion
  slavery
  lying
  perjury

It is obvious that the fruit of the unbeliever's life brings spiritual bondage, while the fruit of the Spirit leads to complete spiritual freedom in Christ. On the surface of things, people may sometimes think that since Christianity makes restrictions it brings bondage; for to some persons restrictions placed on human conduct become an infringement on liberty.

Freedom from restraint, however, leads only to chaos and destruction. Walking in the Spirit, living in the Spirit, or being led by the Spirit may seem restrictive. Yet the Holy Spirit dwelling within the Christian provides the motivation, the power, and the direction the believer needs to be truly free and to bear good fruit.

The work of the Spirit is done secretly and quietly in the heart of the believer. His work includes warning, exhorting, and checking, as well as leading.

The fruit of the Spirit may not be immediately manifested in outward deeds, or even in all the habits of one's life. *The fruit of the Spirit is manifested as a cluster of abilities, qualities, or capacities of the human frame which grow, mature, and develop gradually.*

It is only after the sun has shined, the rain has fallen, and the weeds have been pulled that fruit in the natural realm is evident. Fruitbearing in the Christian life is just as exciting and even more sure while the Christian's relationship is maintained with Christ through the Holy Spirit.

It is clear from the list in this chapter that there is no one passage in the New Testament where all of the various qualities and virtues of the believer's life are brought together to describe fully the Spirit's fruit. In fact, it is probably impossible to enumerate all of the various facets of Christian character in a study of the manifestations of the fruit of the Spirit.

The apostolic writers listed the qualities of character which were especially applicable to their particular readers at the time. From a consideration of the passage cited in each of the above lists, drawn from various epistles by three different apostles, it is clear that there are overlapping and parallel manifestations of the Spirit's work. But there is also distinction and uniqueness.

PRINCIPLES INVOLVED IN FRUITBEARING

Before studying the different qualities of fruit, the following facts should be understood about the manifestation of the Spirit's fruit:

The manifestation of the Spirit's fruit is seen in the fact that those faculties, talents, or capacities which may have been latent, undeveloped, or immature are aroused and put to use.

The manifestation of the Spirit's fruit is seen in the highest level of development in the course of time.

The manifestation of the Spirit's fruit will be seen in the gradual restoration of those faculties, talents, or capacities which have been warped or dwarfed by sin and selfishness.

The manifestation of the fruit of the Spirit, however, goes beyond the restored natural endowments and are seen in spiritual virtues, grace, and qualities which exceed natural capacities.

In this connection S. D. Gordon writes: "It may be said positively that the original group of mental faculties remain the same. There seems to be nothing to indicate that any change takes place in one's natural endowments. No faculty is added that nature has not put there, and certainly none removed.

"But it is very clear that there is a marked development of these natural abilities, and that there is a change brought about by the putting in of a new and tremendous motive power, which radically affects everything it touches."[1]

The following important principles should also be kept in mind as we continue our study:

The Holy Spirit in His production of fruit does not supersede the activity of one's own reason, judgment, moral sense, or will in the practical decisions to be made.

The fruit of the Spirit in its varied manifestations confirms the work of grace the Spirit has done. In this regard the guidance of the Holy Spirit in the conduct of life is not intended to be independent, but comes in connection with the inspired Word of God, one's own common sense, divine providence and the counsel of godly Christian people.

In any manifestation of the work of the Spirit in the believer's life there will be no collision with the Bible. If there is a contradiction with the Scripture in relation to the supposed manifestation of the Spirit, the Scriptures must be accorded authority.

The Holy Spirit creates and conserves holiness in the believer's life. He never leads one into sin or into erroneous doctrines.

Since the Holy Spirit glorifies Christ, He can never disparage Christ's deity or deny His humanity.

It is the work of the Spirit to regenerate and to sanctify; therefore, any substitute to or disparagement of these works of grace cannot be approved of the Spirit, much less inspired by Him.

The conscience of any believer is never in this life an infallible guide to action and conduct. Likewise, the certainty that comes through the direct witness of the Spirit to such works of His grace as adoption and sonship, cannot be carried over in determining the will of God in all areas of everyday life. Intuitive judgments and human reason cannot be removed or disconnected from the sphere of motives, dispositions, and principles. All of these must always be in accord with the revealed Word of God, whose author is the Holy Spirit.

We have noted that vital Christian life, growth, and fruitage are not a cooperative venture. The Holy Spirit does for each person what he cannot do for himself, but the Spirit expects each person to give diligent attention to those things he can do which are conducive to spiritual development.

A PERSON'S ROLE
IN FRUITBEARING

The Apostle Peter shows that each believer has a significant role to play in the abundance and quality of the fruit he will bear.

He indicates that in all earnestness a believer is to build upon his initial faith foundation in Christ. Peter cites (2 Peter 1:5-11, NIV) seven delightful varieties of fruit or Christian graces which are to be built on that foundation by the help of the Holy Spirit as believers diligently cooperate with Him.

First, there is *goodness*. This means moral strength or integrity. Courage is needed in order to profess one's faith before others, especially in the time of persecution such as the Christians of the first century were facing.

Next, there is *knowledge*. That is spiritual and practical discernment which in turn increases one's faith and directs one's courage to the highest ends.

Self-control or temperance is the work of the Spirit whereby a believer maintains his balance. It is the grace whereby in difficult circumstances he successfully withstands temptation. It is that factor by which he not only refuses to do evil, but by which he gives himself to do all possible good. In the self-controlled or disciplined life the physical part of the human nature will not be allowed to subjugate the higher spiritual and rational factors of his being. Self-control also enables the Christian through the help of the Spirit to make the most of the circumstances in which he finds himself.

Perseverance. This is patience, endurance, steadfastness. In the daily tasks and press of life the believer will, by the Spirit, be enabled to bear the difficulties and trials with an even mind and heart.

Yet again, Peter urges the need of *godliness*. This involves a right relationship with God and devotion toward Him. It also is expressed in relationships with and love for all of our fellowmen. The word suggests a deep, reverential religious fear and awe of God.

Brotherly kindness expresses an attitude of love and respect among the people of God. Proper relationships within the body of Christ are imperative for a solid witness to the unbelieving world.

Finally, the capstone is *love*. Here the believer is not pictured in his growth and development totally within the family of God. One's love for all men, even enemies and persecutors, is involved. The devotion and affection for God's cause does not exclude or isolate the Christian from the needs of the human race. Bigotry, selfishness, narrowness, or pettiness cannot exist where the love of God permeates.

Peter states that the cultivation of these graces or virtues are directly related to, if not to be identified as, the fruitfulness of the believer's life. One who possesses the elements enumerated here in increasing measure will never be ineffective and unproductive in his service for the Lord.

On the contrary, fruitfulness and barrenness result from a lack of spiritual growth and diligence in nurturing these virtues. Instead of productiveness, spiritual nearsightedness or blindness follow negligence. One may even forget that past sins have once been cleansed. Tragedy and apostasy are the sure results, just as fruitfulness is certain for the person who cooperates with the grace of God.

James, the half-brother of Jesus, also writes of the result of the work of the Spirit in the Christian's life. James 3:17 speaks of fruitfulness in the following areas:

The *wisdom* to which he refers may rightly be regarded as the fruit of the Spirit, as well as a spiritual gift. In this context the varied elements are itemized which issue from a heavenly or spiritual wisdom.

It is first *pure* or free from selfish emotions, drives, and goals. Purity to the Greeks implied a character pure enough to approach the gods. One's inner life must be open to divine scrutiny if it is to be a fruitbearing life.

To be *peaceable* implies a right relationship between man and man and between man and God. It is opposed to the rude, crude, or violent disposition of those who are disrespectful.

To be *considerate* of and *submissive* to others is sometimes regarded even by the wise men of earth as weaknesses. But such earthly ideas of wisdom do not conform with those of the Holy Spirit. One who is Spirit-filled will exercise gentleness rather than rudeness. Likewise, courtesy is dominant over uncouthness. The fruitbearing Christian will learn to be tolerant and respectful of the feelings of others.

James also urges that wisdom is *open to reason* and will not obstinately cling to its own opinions. To be true to the faith does not call for brusqueness, bitterness, or stubbornness.

Mercy which flows from heavenly wisdom performs every act of kindness within reach. It stands ready to forgive what is intentional as well as what is an accidental transgression of the law of love.

Unity of purpose and singlemindedness are implied in James' use of the term *impartial*. It is a mark of the spiritually wise to render every man his due, without making a difference between persons, and without being swayed by self-interest, worldly honor, or the fear of man.

Although God is the only one who can be absolutely impartial, it is the believer's goal toward which the Spirit will lead him.

Hypocrisy and insincerity are not consistent with the fruit of the Spirit. James shows that a disguise, a mask, or subtility is not a part of heavenly wisdom. An openness and transparency of heart is refreshing in a world of intrigue.

It is evident from these passages that the fruit of the Spirit is not something that just happens. It requires sowing, cultivation, and much labor before a harvest can follow. Everyone enjoys and appreciates the harvest, but too few are willing and prepared to help with the diligent labor required that the Spirit may do His work in the life.

SUMMARY

The presence of the Holy Spirit in the inner life of a believer affects his attitudes and behavior so that the fruit of the Spirit shows outwardly. But the manifestations of that fruit may vary widely because of the differences in the human personalities in and through whom the Spirit works.

The New Testament speaks often of these many varieties of Christian fruitfulness, but nowhere does it bring together all of the possibilities in this area. Perhaps there really is no limit to the variety of fruit which may be produced within the body of Christ, the church, as the Spirit is allowed free course. The New Testament writers did, however, discuss specific graces which were especially applicable or needed in the lives of the particular believers to whom they were writing. Those lists merit our study and prayerful consideration.

What Do You Think About These?

1. Does the fruit of the Spirit show in the life of the believer? Will others notice? How?

2. Why do all Christians not bear fruit in the same measure?

3. What are some factors which affect Christian fruitfulness?

4. What is the greatest of all manifestations of the Spirit's work in our lives?

If You Want to Dig a Little Deeper

1. Without reference to the material in this chapter, list all you can of the qualities or elements of the Spirit's fruit in the believer's life.

2. Compare your list with the tabulation in this chapter.

3. Read all of the passages referred to in the tabulation using several versions of the New Testament, taking note of the various synonyms used to designate the fruit of the Spirit.

4. Read James 3:17; Colossians 1:10, and Philippians 1:11. What truths do you find here?

[1]*Quiet Talks On Power,* p. 23.

RELATIONSHIP WITH GOD:

love, joy,

peace

Relevant Scriptures: Galatians 5:22-23; 2 Peter 1:5-11.

The fruit of the Spirit is, to put it simply, a cluster of Christ's virtues.

This reminds us again that the word *fruit* used as singular noun suggests the united effect of the Spirit's work in the Christian's life. In this sense the fruit of the Spirit is an indivisible cluster of virtues and graces which grow together as the Holy Spirit reproduces Christ's life in the believer.

Some authorities believe that Paul may suggest this in the passage from Galatians we will now consider. They feel that love is actually the fruit of the Spirit and that love is joyful, serene, patient, kind, good, faithful, gentle, and self-controlled.

In this regard S. D. Gordon suggests that joy is love singing, peace is love resting, patience is love enduring, kindness is love sharing, goodness is love's integrity, faithfulness is love's habit, gentleness is love's touch, and self-control is love in full charge.

However we may look at it, love is an essential element wherever the Spirit is at work. But here we will treat love as one of the nine elements of the Spirit's fruit. We shall consider these elements as three triads (group of three) relating to personal, social, and virtuous-dynamic character.

In this section we think particularly about the first triad: love, joy, and peace. These naturally and logically pertain directly to one's inner relationship with God. Let us consider the triad in the sequence of the passage.

LOVE

The Bible does not define love. But it does provide scores of illustrations which help us understand it.

Love is holiness, purity of heart in action. The Bible teaches us that:

Love is exercised and demonstrated in a concern for the poor.[1] Love is seen in one's honest transaction of business.[2] Love is manifested in one's purity of speech.[3] Love is shown by a proper respect for God's name. [4] Love is projected by carefulness in payment of wages.[5] Love is portrayed by care and understanding of the handicapped.[6]

God has given us many examples of His love in the Bible as well as throughout His created universe. Jesus taught His followers to love their enemies as He did. He stated that God's enemies enjoy sunshine and rain just as do those who serve Him. The Christian, when confronted by perverted and repulsive individuals, needs to remember this. God loves even the most unlovely person.

The Apostle Paul tells Christians: "Be kind and compassionate to one another, forgiving each other, just as in Christ God forgave you" (Ephesians 4:32, NIV). If we were treated by Christ as we may have treated others at times, where would any of us be? Love is in harmony with God's way.

Love is from God, for God is love. "We love him, because he first loved us" (1 John 4:19). Paul indicates that love is the quality which binds together all other Christian virtues. He wrote: "Put on love, which binds them all together in perfect unity" (Colossians 3:14, NIV). This is in accord with the perfect unity and oneness of God's own person, nature, and being. The expression of God's love is best seen in John 3:16: "God so loved the world, that he gave his only begotten Son, that whosoever believeth in him should not perish, but have everlasting life."

The love of God is the source and standard of love in man. "Herein is love, not that we loved God, but that he loved us, and sent his Son to be the propitiation for our sins" (1 John 4:10).

Although the word *love* is used in various ways in the New Testament, the Greek term *agape* is used by Paul in Galatians to express love as the fruit of the Spirit. It is the general word used in the New Testament to distinguish divine love from human love.

When agape love is in a person's heart, he will seek the highest good of others. There may at times be emotion with *agape* love, but it is not necessary to it. *This kind of love is more than emotion.* It is love that gives, that sacrifices, that has compassion. The believer's will determines and controls the expression of this love. It is active and wills to love when people deserve it and even when they do not. It builds good relationships and helps, whatever the outcome.

J. K. Grider relates an experience when a little waif of a girl spat in the face of his small child as they played in the backyard. His first reaction upon seeing the spiteful act was to send the violator on her way so as never to return. But then he remembered that the little girl came from a broken home and lived with friends nearby, and needed love. He talked with her and walked with her in the yard for a while. She must have sensed, even at her tender age, the concern and love Mr. Grider felt for her, for the next day there was a light rap at his door. He answered it. At the door stood the little girl. Without a word she placed a handful of crumpled flowers, mostly petals, in his hand. Then she was gone. Love had been reciprocated on the human level, if not the divine.

Love is unceasingly active on behalf of others. *Love is the opposite of selfishness.* It lives for others. It motivates one to serve.

Christian love is not simply a product of the human heart when one wills it, however. *Love is a divine fruit made real to us and others by the agency of the Holy Spirit.*

Christian love differs from human love in that it includes the entire person: heart, mind, will, feelings. It triumphs over self. The unbeliever has no way to experience this love. Only when repentance and reconciliation with God come through faith and obedience can love begin to pour in from God by His Holy Spirit.

JOY

Joy is closely associated with love. It is a manifestation in the personal life of fruit provided by the Holy Spirit. It surpasses human experience and understanding.

Everyone has known the delight of meeting a long-set goal or deadline, of seeing a great work of art, or sharing a fine experience. This form of human satisfaction is more appropriately called happiness, because it is based on happenings, circumstances, or motivational factors. Our human nature provides for the pleasant feelings associated with the fulfillment of wants, needs, or values.

But the fruit of the Spirit known as joy is more than happiness. It is a comfort which continues even in the face of distress, and provides hope even in the face of failure. Joy is not destroyed by circumstances or happenings.

"It is a basic attitude or habit of mind that springs from the depth of the soul, where all is right because Christ is King and life is full of the Spirit," says W. T. Dayton.

It is true that Christians encounter sorrow. There are many instances of it in the Bible. The saints wept at Miletus when the Ephesian elders understood that they would not see Paul again in this life.[7] Paul felt deep sorrow until he knew that Epaphroditus had been healed.[8] Both Jesus and Paul wept when they thought of the rebellion and obstinacy of unbelief.[9] Peter reminded Christians that they would always be subject to sorrows because of the treatment they could expect from the world.[10]

Nevertheless, the Bible teaches that Christians possess an abiding joy. James states that even temptation is a reason for rejoicing.[11] Although Paul was in prison, he rejoiced in God's grace.[12] Paul and John were full of joy upon hearing of their converts.[13] Paul urges Christians to rejoice under any and all kinds of occasions.[14]

Such joy can have its origin only in God. It is the joy of the Holy Spirit produced as one trusts in Christ.[15] It is based on the reality of God and in infallible promises of His Word. It is the positive knowledge that God's will is being done.

Christ is said to have promised His disciples three things: They would be completely fearless, in constant trouble, but absurdly joyful! The first-century Christians must have found the truth of this, for the word "joy" is used more than 60 times in the New Testament, and "rejoice" is used at least 72 times. Indeed, the New Testament begins with angels giving voice to good news of great joy to all people, and ends with joy filling heaven!

Like love, joy is not mere emotion. It is love smiling, not necessarily by facial expression but in the heart. It is the inward reality which produces an outward radiance because of one's relationship to Jesus Christ through the Holy Spirit. The believer's relationship with Christ is what counts and lasts!

Before leaving His disciples, Jesus said, "These things I have spoken to you, that my joy may be in you, and that your joy may be full" (John 15:11, NASB). The Gospels repeatedly picture Jesus as filled with sorrow, but also full of joy. The gospel which Jesus lived and preached actually means good, or joyful news.

John Wesley states that "sour godliness is the devil's religion." No one serves God better by being sad rather than glad. Jesus gave three cheers to the Christian: "Be of good cheer, thy sins be forgiven" (Matthew 9:2). "Be of good cheer, it is I, be not afraid" (Mark 6:50). "Be of good cheer, I have overcome the world" (John 16:33). Here are the cheers for forgiveness, for companionship, and for victory in Christ!

The fruit of *joy has the Holy Spirit of God as both its source and as its object.* The psalmist asserts this when he declares, "In thy presence is fulness of joy; at thy right hand there are pleasures for evermore" (Psalm 16:11). Joy is as natural to the Spirit-filled Christian as beauty to a rose or a song to a bird. Joy comes in doing God's will and in living in His presence.

To know God's will and to do it brings the highest joy on earth. It is heaven on earth. *One reason some Christians may lose the radiance and joy of their Christian experience is because they do not seek actively to serve others.*

One man asked his pastor what he could do to regain the joy he once knew. His pastor, handing him an address on a slip of paper, said, "Go to the grocery store and buy $50.00 worth of groceries and take them to the poor family at this address. Then stay and visit with them, find out what more they need, pray with them, then go get what more they need." Love serving brings joy. Like all fruit, it needs cultivating.

People who try to appear righteous are quite often joyless people, because they are pretending. People who are led and filled with the Spirit radiate the fullness of joy. It comes naturally from within.

Another distinction may be noted concerning the Spirit's fruit of joy. *Joy's outward expression is praise.* A fresh awareness of the joy of the Lord issues in praise, praise to God and appreciation of one's fellowmen. The greatest in the kingdom of God may not be the one who prays most, or fasts most often, or gives most, but the one who praises God most for His goodness, mercy, and love. All the other things will be added to the praiseful heart overflowing with the joy of the Lord.

Praise is love and joy at work. It opens the eyes of faith and hope. It not only honors God, it lifts man from the wilderness of worry and complaint. The day before John Wesley died he sang Isaac Watts's hymn, "I'll praise my Maker while I've breath, And when my voice is lost in death, Praise shall employ my nobler powers."

Many saints through the ages have followed the example of Paul and Silas in the Philippian jail when they sang praises to God at midnight. Isaiah had the basis of it all when he wrote that God would give "beauty for ashes, the oil of joy for mourning, the garment of praise for the spirit of heaviness" (Isaiah 61:3).

Those who are bearing the fruit of the Spirit will make a "joyful noise unto the Lord," will "sing forth the honor of his name," and will "make his praise glorious" (Psalm 66:1-2).

PEACE

Peace has at least two important bases in the New Testament. First, it comes from faith and trust in God. Paul wrote to the Romans, "May the God of hope fill you with all joy and peace *as you trust* in him, so that you may overflow with hope by the power of the Holy Spirit" (Romans 15:13, NIV). It is "peace with God through the Lord Jesus Christ" (Romans 5:1). Peace comes when one trusts and believes what God has revealed through His Son.

Second, peace comes when belief is turned to action. It is not merely passive, but active *obedience* to what God wills. These bases (trust and obedience) give support to the conclusion that peace is a very personal quality. The song "Trust and Obey" certainly comes to mind as an illustration of these two bases.

A troubled person will trouble a community. Similarly, peace comes to a community as it comes to individuals in a personal way within that community.

Isaiah pointed out that there is no peace to the wicked. Until Christ effects a reconciliation in a person's life, the breach between God and man remains. When peace is made with God, a relationship is established which involves a person's character. This is not merely a psychological adjustment, though it does involve one's mind and thoughts. It is not simply a sorting out of pressures or disturbances from the workaday world, although that may be helpful and meaningful. It is basically and primarily spiritual, thus a fruit of the Spirit's work and indwelling.

The biblical use of peace, although very diverse and broad, is set forth most clearly in the character and works of God. It is the "God of peace [who will] bruise Satan under your feet shortly" (Romans 16:20). It is also the "God of peace [who will] sanctify you wholly" (1 Thessalonians 5:23). And it was the "God of peace that brought again from the dead our Lord Jesus" (Hebrews 13:20). Christ also promised, "Peace I leave with you: my peace I give to you" (John 14:27).

Peace is "the calm, quiet, and order which takes place in the justified soul instead of the doubts, fears, alarms, and dreadful forebodings which every true penitent feels, and must feel until the assurance of pardon brings peace and satisfaction to the mind" (Adam Clarke).

Peace is not an achievement so much as a relationship. It is a harmonious relationship with one's Creator so that His creatures may also be in harmony. Peace as a fruit of the Spirit quells, even extinguishes, the war and conflict which rages within the human life left to its natural course. It provides a rest, a tranquillity, a freedom from strain and drain inherent in anxiety or worry.

Peace is pictured by an artist's drawing. It was a picture of a thundering waterfall. Beside it was a tree, a branch of which hung far out over the tumbling cataract. Upon the limb a bird had built a nest and was hovering over small nestlings.

So peace is not detachment from the roaring turbulence of life's cares and concerns. It fully recognizes them, it exists in their very presence, and yet displays calm courage.

Nothing describes the will and work of God through His Son more accurately than the phrase from Isaiah 9, "Prince of Peace." That appellation forecast the angels' message at the Messiah's birth and also one of the last words of direction that Christ gave to His disciples, three times repeated, "Peace be with you" (John 20:19-21, 26).

Peace, then, as the fruit of the Spirit is first of all peace with God. Peace flows from forgiveness in Christ. Peace results from undeviating devotion to God's will. Peace comes from confidence in God's promises. "Let us therefore follow after the things which make for peace, and things wherewith one may edify another" (Romans 14:19) while we "follow peace with all men, and holiness, without which no man shall see the Lord" (Hebrews 12:14).

SUMMARY

The Holy Spirit is the Spirit of Jesus; and in the life of the believer He produces the virtues which Christ demonstrated among men.

The Apostle Paul in Galatians 5:22-23 lists nine of those virtues which can well be divided into three groups in that each of the three groups relates to a different aspect of Christian living. The first triad — love, joy, peace — has to do especially with one's personal *inner relationship with God.* The second — long-suffering, gentleness, goodness — has to do especially with our *relationship with other persons.* The third group — faithfulness, meekness, self-control — has to do with what we are in *relation to ourselves,* qualities of character which make for dynamic Christian living.

Love which comes from God is holiness or purity of heart in action. The *joy* of the Lord is a source of strength at all times. Not dependent upon circumstances, it is present even amid distress and failure. *Peace* which the Spirit gives is first of all peace with God. This is reflected though in peace with ourselves and with our fellowmen.

What Do You Think About These?

1. What is agape love?

2. What is the opposite of love — hate? Selfishness?

3. Can you love a person yet not *like* them?

4. What is the difference between joy and happiness?

5. Is it true that real peace means retreating from the storms of life — like going to a monastery?

If You Want to Dig a Little Deeper

1. Can you list five examples from Scripture which show love in action?

2. What is the significance of regarding the fruit of the Spirit as a cluster?

Bible References Relating to This Chapter

[1]Leviticus 19:9-10; Deuteronomy 24:19-22; James 2:1-7, 14-17.

[2]Psalm 15; Proverbs 20:7-14.

[3]Leviticus 19:16: Psalm 19:14; 51:15; Matthew 12:33-37.

[4]Exodus 20:7; Leviticus 19:12; Matthew 5:33-37; Luke 11:2; Philippians 2:9-11.

[5]Leviticus 19:13; Deuteronomy 24:15; Luke 12:15; 1 Timothy 6:9-10, 17-18; James 5:4.

[6]Leviticus 19:14; Deuteronomy 27:18; Acts 3:1-10.

[7]Acts 20:36-38.   [15]Romans 14:17; 15:13.

[8]Philippians 2:27.

[9]Luke 19:41; Romans 9:2.

[10]1 Peter 2:19.

[11]James 1:2.

[12]Philippians 1:18.

[13]Philippians 1:3-5; 4:10; 2 John 4.

[14]Philippians 4:4; 1 Thessalonians 5:16.

RELATIONSHIP WITH OTHERS:
long-suffering, kindness, goodness

4

Relevant Scripture: Galatians 5:22-23.

"It was not Livingstone's preaching that converted me. It was Livingstone's living." That is the way newsman and explorer Henry Stanley summarized the influence of the famous missionary upon him.

After finding David Livingstone in central Africa and spending four months with him there, Stanley declared, "I went to Africa as prejudiced as the biggest atheist in London. But there came a long time for reflection. I saw this solitary old man there and asked myself, 'How on earth does he stay here? What is it that inspires him?' For months I found myself wondering at the old man carrying out all that was said in the Bible 'Leave all things and follow.' But little by little my sympathy was aroused. Seeing his piety, his gentleness, his zeal, his earnestness I was converted by him, although he had not tried to do it!"

That's the way it is with the fruitbearing Christian life. It wins — wins others.

Because this is true, we come to understand that the Holy Spirit applies the benefits of Christ's redemptive ministry to one's relationship to others, as well as to the character of the individual believer himself. The social outworkings of the Spirit's indwelling are indeed amazing and marvelous.

The second triad of spiritual fruit looks outward to the believer's neighbors and all of his fellowmen. Love will outwardly express itself in many ways as the Holy Spirit is permitted His perfect work in one's social life.

LONG-SUFFERING

The word used for the first social quality of spiritual fruit comes from two words meaning literally, "long" and "soul" or "spirit." The word is very strong and suggests that the whole inner man is involved.

Long-suffering is patience under trial. It is a protracted restraint of the soul from yielding to passion, especially the passion of anger.

It has also been said that it is "the brave patience with which the Christian contends against the various hindrances, persecutions, and temptations that befall him in his conflict with the inward and outward world."

God reveals in varied texts that long-suffering is a quality of His own person and nature.[1] So it is that the God of patience and forbearance imparts patience and long-suffering to His children.

This is love manifested under pressure or injuries inflicted by others. It is "long-mindedness, bearing with the frailties and provocations of others, from the consideration that God has borne long with ours and that, if He had not, we should have been speedily consumed; bearing up also through all the troubles and difficulties of life without murmuring or repining; submitting cheerfully to every dispensation of God's providence, and thus deriving benefit from every occurrence." — Adam Clarke

Our patience in the Spirit does not imply an uneasy, clock-watching, floor-pacing, deep-sighing endurance test. It is patience based on a respect for the other person, a genuine love for him, and a willingness to sacrifice time or life's energies for him.

When one begins to run low on joy or peace, impatience will not be far behind. The world is full of pressures because of sin, and God's people are not immune from temptations to impatience. It is only through the power of the Spirit that long-suffering will come through the believer's life to others.

Some observations have been noted concerning the interrelatedness of the fruit of the Spirit. Nowhere is this more evident than in long-suffering or patience. It does not stand alone. It is supported by and supports other Christian virtues.

Peter wanted to put a limit on patience when he asked the Master, "How oft shall my brother sin against me, and I forgive him?" (Matthew 18:21). Jesus' reply to Peter shows that patience is such a powerful force in God's nature that it cannot be measured; and in the Christian's life which is filled with the Spirit there should be no desire or disposition to measure it.

James gives three examples of patience which point up its importance. There is the *patience of the farmer.* "See how the farmer waits for the land to yield its valuable crop and how patient he is for the fall and spring rains" (James 5:7, NIV). Every farmer knows that the time of harvest cannot be hurried. He must submit to the laws of maturation. The analogy in the spiritual world is in steadfast obedience to God and His timetable for our lives. It implies a trust in God when events occur which seem wasteful, senseless, or useless.

Then there is the example of *the prophets' patience.* "As an example of patience in the face of suffering, take the prophets who spoke in the name of the Lord" (James 5:10, NIV). A martyr suffers because of good behavior, not evil. He bears fruit or has his reward only because and when he bears it patiently.[2]

Finally, there is the *patience of Job*. "You have heard of Job's perseverance and have seen what the Lord finally brought about" (James 5:11, NIV). God did not tell Job all that he would have liked to have known about his situation. Had he known as God knew, and as God showed him when he was vindicated, Job would have been greatly comforted. This shows that God may not place great importance on knowledge in a given situation, but rather He is concerned that we trust Him and hang on in order that the Holy Spirit may do His perfect work in us.

Patience is not merely passive. It is active and strong. It is power. It is love suffering long.[3] It has a calm anticipation and hope for a change for the better in one's fellowman. Patience is a preeminent quality of the Spirit's fruit. "It is not clad with glamour or romance; it is not the excitement of sudden adventurous action; but it is the very virtue of God himself." — William Barclay. God, for example, does not abandon hope of the earth He has created, even though more often than not the people he placed here turn their backs on Him.

It is obvious that impetuous Peter, among all of the apostles, may have been most in need of this grace of patience. He apparently learned his lesson. In his epistle he wrote, "The Lord . . .

is long-suffering . . . not willing that any should perish, but that all should come to repentance" (2 Peter 3:9).

Long-suffering and forbearance are clearly synonymous with patience. These qualities make for a moral strength which absorbs blow after blow on the anvil of life. The fruit of the Spirit which enables a believer to remain calm and quiet no matter what the circumstances is sure to be manifested in one's social relationships.

KINDNESS

Kindness is one of the greatest social graces.

Kindness is sensitivity to the feelings of others. It guards against the needless injury or hurt of another person in any manner. It is not, however, contrary to firmness and courage. Courtesy and consideration are constituent elements in kindness.

Prince Edward of Wales entertained an Indian prince who was not acquainted with all of the Western rules of etiquette. When the Indian saw a finger bowl at his plate, he assumed the water in it was to drink, which he promptly did. Before anyone had opportunity to raise an eyebrow or grin, the Prince of Wales lifted his finger bowl and did likewise.

One could not assume from this fact that Prince Edward was filled with the Spirit, but it illustrates that one who is bearing the fruit of kindness is considerate of others' feelings.

Christians will try to cover the faults and sins of others with love and kindness. In fact, there are numerous references in Scripture to love and kindness used together in the word "loving-kindness."[4]

This is a reminder that the Scripture is presenting Christian character as of one fabric. Inevitably one trait or element blends into all the others.

Kindness is not characterized by a saccharine sweetness that covers hostility with flattery. It is not an attempt to manipulate someone into helping us. Rather, it is a sincere desire to help another person bear his burdens.

Selfishness and pride are not consistent with this or any other part of Christian fruit. At the same time, not all people are unkind, naturally. And all persons are not unkind all of the time. Jacob showed kindness to Esau, but, nevertheless, deprived him of his birthright.[5] Jael gave Sisera a bottle of milk just before he took a little nap, but she literally "nailed" him.[6] Delilah spoke soothing words of love to Samson but thereby sapped him of his power.[7]

All of these acts were, of course, deceptive and were not conceived by the Spirit, but by human craftiness.

"Kindness is love active." Henry Drummond wrote, "The greatest thing a man can do for His Heavenly Father is to be kind to some of His other children . . . I shall pass through this life but once. Any good thing therefore that I can show to any human being, let me do it now. Let me not defer it or neglect it, for I shall not pass this way again."

Adam Clarke states that kindness is a very rare grace. It is affability and benignity. "A good education and polished manners, when brought under the influence of the grace of God, will bring out this grace with great effect."

Kindness is both active and passive. It may be expressed either in the arena of patient endurance or in the everyday habit of usefulness. It is not hard to live with, and there are no boundaries for its expression.

Kindness is awareness and consideration of the feelings and needs of others. It seeks to understand the other person, even in wrongdoing. Tenderheartedness and forgiveness are in accord with kindness.

Kindness is not weakness. It is not a shallow niceness. A weak Christian is often characterized by harsh criticism and by unkindness or intolerance of others' opinions that vary from his own. The strong Christian is the most kind, for the Spirit of Christ is generous, kind, and friendly.

Kindness builds togetherness. It is thoughtfulness put into action. It is love manifest in little things. It gives a healing touch and avoids evil speaking of others. It looks for opportunities to serve and to be helpful. There is only one letter difference in the Greek between Christ (*Christos*) and kindness (*chrestos*).

There is often a difference between the way a Christian relates to and works with those who are closest, such as the members of his own family, and others with whom he works. One little child prayed that her mother would be as nice to the family at home as she was to the customers she served each day at the store where she worked.

Kindness is a language the deaf can hear and the blind can see. It is needed everywhere and can be practiced anywhere. The Master made an amazing claim for kindness. When a cup of cold water is given in His name, it is really given to Him (Matthew 25:40).

A college professor asked the members of his class to choose the person on campus whom they disliked most and then every day perform some act of kindness toward that person. At the end of one month persons in the class were transformed as well as were many of those who received their kindness.

One writer has observed that when God speaks He usually speaks through a human person who shows kindness. Unkindness, criticism, and coldness will dry up the wellspring of God's spiritual fruit in anyone's life! Kindness is the voice of communication of the Spirit which everyone understands.

GOODNESS

Goodness is a translation of a New Testament Greek word which means also profitableness, wholesomeness, and kindness. That goodness and kindness are closely allied there can be no question. But the shades of difference are worthy of notice.

Bishop Lightfoot thinks that goodness is the energizing force behind kindness.

Goodness is certainly an attribute of God. This is illustrated in the case of the young ruler's question put to Jesus in Luke 18:18, NASB, when he began by saying, "Good Master." Jesus' response was, "Why do you call me good? No one is good except God." Jesus did not deny that the word applied to Him, but it seems that He wanted the young ruler to know that only God was good in the absolute sense of the word. Any goodness that man has is only relative.

Although relative, goodness is nevertheless real, for God's goodness is communicated to the believer as a fruit of the Spirit's inner presence. Goodness well describes the character of a regenerated person in his social relationships.

In Romans 15:14, NASB, Paul states that his readers were "full of goodness," that they were "filled with all knowledge," and that they were "able . . . to admonish one another." What Paul seems to be teaching is that goodness and knowledge are needed in order to administer correction or to give constructive criticism. It is only the mature who can give and take the kind of frank discussion that leads to increased fruitfulness and effectiveness. Abigail had this ability when she delivered David from almost certainly committing murder.[8] Likewise, Paul was effective in his open rebuke of Peter who was frustrating the gospel's impact at Antioch by his narrow and cowardly practice.[9]

John Wesley wrote of goodness: "it means all that is benign, soft, winning, tender, either in temper or behaviour." Peter and Luke agree that goodness was a quality of the life of both Jesus and a man like Barnabas. Of Jesus Peter said, "He went about doing good" (Acts 10:38, NASB), and of Barnabas Luke wrote, "He was a good man" (Acts 11:24).

Although good deeds can be done and may be cited without reference to the work of the Holy Spirit, it is impossible to presume the concept of goodness without bringing the character of the person into the picture.

Goodness deals with motives and purposes toward others in society. *Good* and *God* are related in their English etymology and mean strong, pure, holy, and sincere. Therefore, goodness and godliness are the sum total of personal righteousness.

Goodness implies hidden sources of communication and conduct for the benevolence of mankind. It involves liberality of spirit, the disposition to be magnanimous. It may also be translated as generosity. Goodness does not calculate the cost of service rendered. It works whether appreciation is given or not. It is not the result of self-struggle to do right. It is what God works in the believer through His Spirit.

Goodness involves the courage to care and to understand. The courage to care and to understand is the basis of all effective communication with need. A world traveler projected a series of pictures which depicted serious need. One little girl was pictured with her face pressed hard against the windowpane on the inside of which was an abundance of food. The girl was weak and frail from lack of food. When asked what he had done about the little girl's need, the traveler's reply was, "Oh, I was simply taking pictures of the world need!"

Goodness will assuredly be evidenced in a life of good deeds, which in turn are known generally as kindness. Goodness is the quality which becomes active in kindness and both are the genuine fruit of the Spirit, inextricably woven together with love, joy, peace, and long-suffering.

SUMMARY

The fruitbearing believer is bound to influence and win other persons. He not only enjoys the love, joy, and peace of God within himself, but he manifests toward others an attitude characterized by long-suffering, kindness, and goodness. Those qualities speak for themselves and loudly.

Long-suffering or patience are moral and spiritual strengths which enable the believer to absorb blow after blow on life's anvil. The assurance and quietness they produce under all circumstances cannot but affect all of one's social relationships.

Kindness, sensitivity to, and regard for the feelings of other persons, is a warm, powerful force, which goes a long way to counteract much of the cold unconcern which dominates our society. The showing of concern, really caring, and manifesting it by kindness is very often the channel through which God reaches those in need of His love and salvation.

Goodness is indeed an inner quality of spirit, but in the life of a Christian it reflects to others the God who is the source of all goodness in the earth.

This triad — long-suffering, kindness, and goodness — provides the major characteristics through which Christians may expect to influence and win others. In manifesting these qualities they become the salt of the earth, the light of the world.

What Do You Think About These?

1. Develop a simple, easy-to-remember definition of: long-suffering, kindness, goodness.

2. Among your acquaintances think of specific acts which have seemed to reflect each of these qualities.

3. What Bible examples of each of these qualities can you think of?

For Those Who Wish to Dig a Little Deeper

1. How do you reconcile these qualities of life with the anger Christians should have toward evil? Do you see a reconciliation of these in Jesus' life?

2. What does 1 Corinthians 13:4 say to you regarding the unity existing between these three qualities and the three qualities in the previous session?

Bible References Relating to This Chapter

[1]Luke 18:7; Romans 15:5; 1 Peter 3:20; 2 Peter 3:9, 15.

[2]1 Peter 2:19-20; 3:17.

[3]1 Corinthians 13:4.

[4]Psalms 17:7; 25:6; 26:3; 36:7, 10; 40:10-11; 42:8; 48:9; 51:1; 63:3; 69:16; 88:11; 89:33, 49; 92:2; 103:4; 107:43; 119:88, 149, 159; 138:2; 143:8;

Isaiah 63:7, 9, et. al.
[5]Genesis 25:34.
[6]Judges 4:18ff.
[7]Judges 16:4ff.
[8]1 Samuel 25:34.
[9]Galatians 2:11-16.

RELATIONSHIP WITH SELF: faithfulness, meekness, self-control

5

Relevant Scriptures: Psalm 89: Galatians 5:22-23.

Each of us ultimately will be judged by what we did for and to other persons; but that judgment will as surely involve what each of us has made of himself in the light of what he might have become. How fully I am reaching my potential for God and good is a question we all need to face up to. This is where such things as faithfulness and self-control come in. They have a great deal to do in determining the kind of person each of us will become, what our character will be.

This kind of thinking brings us to the final triad of the Spirit's fruit which Paul depicts in Galatians 5:22-23. Paul ends his catalog on a very positive note with three virtues which are capstones to all else. The point is that conduct cannot exemplify the fruit of the Spirit unless it issues from character.

FAITHFULNESS

Most authorities agree that the New Testament Greek word here is not best translated "faith," as in the King James Version, but rather as "faithfulness." That faithfulness is based on faith, there can be no doubt, but here it is the conduct, the dynamic of faith in action that Paul is portraying.

Faith and trust in God issue in trustworthiness, honesty, fidelity, and dependability. The writer of the book of Hebrews pictures Christ as an example of this quality. He writes, ". . . consider Jesus, the Apostle and High Priest of our confession. He was faithful to Him who appointed Him, as Moses also was in all his house" (Hebrews 3:1-2).

The term expresses the idea of fidelity. It is demonstrated in ". . . punctuality in performing promises, conscientious carefulness in preserving what is committed to our trust, in restoring it to its proper owner, in transacting the business confided to us, neither betraying the secret of our friend nor disappointing the confidence of our employer." — Adam Clarke

Faithfulness is a dependability that never gives up or lets down. It is impossible to imagine Christ ever letting anyone down or giving up in His purpose and mission.

But too many Christians give up too soon or let down too quickly. Pastors are let down by members, and members are let down by pastors. The teacher of a Sunday school class is let down when members do not attend, and the members of the class are let down when the teacher is not there. Choir members who show up only occasionally are not faithful.

Jesus was utterly faithful. He is the same yesterday, today, and forever. Faithfulness. Dependability. Reliability. This is the fruit of the Spirit!

Faithfulness flows from faith in God. When the believer's attention is focused in Him, steadiness and dependability develop. Not all at once, but gradually. That is why Paul could say at the end of his life, "I have fought a good fight, I have finished my course, I have kept the faith" (2 Timothy 4:7).

● One of the best examples of the scope of faithfulness is in the description of God's own faithfulness in Psalm 89. The following aspects of God's faithful character are cited:

● He is faithful to all generations. It is not an occasional or whimsical part of His care for His creatures.

● His faithfulness is as firm as the heavens; and so is not subject to the changes which occur among men.

● His faithfulness is to be declared in the assembly of the believers.

● His faithfulness is combined with His power

and might so that nothing can divert Him from His purposes.

● His faithfulness is combined with his righteousness and justice as foundations of His throne.

● His faithfulness is combined with His steadfast love in at least six different cases.

● His faithfulness is not made null and void by the faithlessness of His creatures.

● His faithfulness is not obscured when He chastens His people. It is rather because of His steadfast love and faithfulness that He disciplines.

Observing God's faithfulness should teach us that a believer will bear the same fruit of the Spirit in a relative measure.

The believer's faithfulness is not to be occasional, related to circumstances. Circumstances should not deter one from his purpose to be a blessing to mankind. The Christian who bears this fruit does not rest his dependability upon the presence of or the absence of faithfulness in another person. Even if visible supports are taken away, the believer has a reserve in God that causes this fruit to continue unabated.

It should also be noted that there is a correlation between obedience and faithfulness. When one determines to obey God, faithful actions follow naturally. There is also a direct correlation between a person's faithfulness and his attitude toward God, his sense of the importance of the gospel, and the reality of the Second Coming of Christ.

Faithfulness speaks of firmness of purpose, of endurance, especially during test, trial, danger, and calamity. It is not a passive attitude or a "grin and bear it" position. It is a careful discharge of obligations. Veracity and honesty are implied.

The final question of God at judgment time may well be, not how much has a person done or how much has he been noticed, but if the believer has been faithful to the calling and to the task assigned by the Heavenly Father. *Christians are not called to be famous or successful, but faithful.* W. T. Purkiser notes that "faithfulness and success are not necessarily related one to another."

A question which should concern the believer is that one asked by Jesus, "When the Son of man cometh, shall he find faith on the earth?" (Luke 18:8). It will most certainly be found as a fruit of the Spirit in the lives of those who are attached to the vine and are growing in grace.

MEEKNESS

Some translations correctly render this word, "gentleness." *It is only the person of strength who can afford, from a human standpoint, to be meek under pressure.* Since meekness is the absence of weakness, a weak person is not gentle and mild but must make up for his weakness by ruthless, rude projections.

Just as self-centeredness produces violence, so meekness and gentleness are produced as a fruit of the Spirit expressing a quality of Christ's own character. No one can have their true self-esteem in proper perspective without the help of the Spirit. The natural self will perpetrate weakness rather than strength of character.

Meekness arises from a proper understanding of ourselves. It also gives insight into the needs of others. Paul states that the Lord's servant must ". . . be gentle unto all men, apt to teach, patient. In meekness instructing those that oppose themselves, . . ." (2 Timothy 2:24-25).

Meekness is "mildness, indulgence toward the weak and erring, patient suffering of injuries without feeling a spirit of revenge, *an even balance of all tempers and passions,* the opposite of anger." — Adam Clarke

The modern world sets a high premium on self-assertiveness. Jesus' beatitude would be re-written: "Blessed are the strong, the shrewd, those who stand up for their rights, those who do not let anyone take advantage of them, those who look out for slights of men, and those who make a success of life."

The Greek word here was used in relation to an animal which had been trained by its master. Wild and unruly animals, after long periods of training, were taught to be gentle. Although their nature was not changed, at least their conduct could be redirected. Thus a horse was tamed and controlled by the bridle.[1] The use of the word "gentleman" is based on the same idea that the man being spoken of has a gentle manner, is courteous and kind.

Christian meekness is strength of character, the base of right conduct, under control of God's Holy Spirit as a fruit unto holiness. It is an attitude toward God which manifests itself also toward one's fellows. The meek who accept God's will and dealings without sulking, murmuring, rebellion, and resistance, are gentle toward other persons.

It should also be noted that the meek person does not hesitate to take strong action when righteousness demands it. William Barclay ends a discussion of meekness by writing that meekness ". . . is the complete control of the passionate part of our nature. It is when we have meekness that we treat all men with perfect courtesy, that we can rebuke without rancour, that we can argue without intolerance, that we can face the truth without resentment, that we can be angry and yet sin not, that we can be gentle and yet not weak."

Why was Jesus confident in saying of himself, "Learn of me, for I am meek and lowly in heart" (Matthew 11:29)? It was precisely because He did not seek His own glory,[2] He did not

receive glory from men,[3] He could do nothing of himself,[4] and He did not come to do His own will.[5]

Gentleness is one of the strongest forces in the world, for it is an element of love. It is love's sweet voice and manner. Only the meek can do the work of restoration.[6]

It is the gentle Christian who restores the fallen one. The meek help others to God. They bring out the best in others. They give others a second chance.

Sometimes meekness is contrasted with pride. It is likewise often identified with humility. When gentleness and humility are properly related, they are seen as arising from an undeserved and unearned relationship with their Creator God who is the very essence of all such virtues. When Joseph Parker was asked why Jesus chose Judas to be one of His disciples, his reply was that he didn't know. But he said, "I have a much harder question. 'Why did He choose me?' "

The meek and humble spirit is a teachable one. The late E. Stanley Jones stated that he had learned to profit by the criticism of others. He asked himself first if the criticism were true. If it was, he applied it to the point of need. If it was not, it was still useful to keep the fires of love burning. In either event, his critic became "the unpaid watchman of my soul."

The world of ordinary men consider the

meek as weak. They are the ones who do not shove and push or shout for revenge. They can be elbowed out of the way because they count for so little by the world's values. But the world is mistaken. The Master said that the "meek shall inherit the earth." Heirs of this world may get title deeds and see huge accounts in the bank grow. But the meek possess the greatest wealth of all by entering into the richest, fullest, freest life which God has promised to His own.

SELF-CONTROL

Moderation in eating, drinking, sleeping, and even in working is to exercise self-control. This fruit suggests continence and self-government especially "with regard to sensual or animal appetites," according to Adam Clarke.

Self-control "is the crowning glory of life in the Spirit. To the renewed image of God in the redeemed is added the renewal prerogative of dominion. Since, on the human level, all legitimate control begins with self-control, here is the solid base for trustworthy service." — Wilber T. Dayton

God does not make puppets out of us or take away control from us. He rather restores control of ourselves which was lost by the Fall and gives His Holy Spirit as our empowerment.

Self-control, like all of the qualities of the Spirit's fruit, is not simply a passive ascetic pose, but implies discipline and positive action directed by the Holy Spirit.

Fire, water, and wind are all immeasurably useful when under control and within boundaries of service to God's creatures. But any of these out of control do vast damage and bring needless suffering. Men may not always be able to control each of these necessary elements of nature, but he has been given the responsibility of working at the job. And when it comes to one's own personal capacities and abilities, life can never be better than when he exercises self-control or self-discipline with the help of the Holy Spirit, whether that pertains to his body, his mind, or his soul.

Self-control is last in the list of the Spirit's fruit, not because it is least, but because it ties all the rest together. The Greeks had a fine idea and goal when they said, "know thyself," but Christ had the best when He taught His disciples to "rule yourself."

Self-control is not just getting hold of one's self or sitting on one's passions by sheer determination. It is a fruit of the Spirit which grows by surrendering to Christ and committing our way to the Holy Spirit. Not only is the desire for self-control present, but the power is given to discipline one's whole being. Paul could encourage Timothy in this truth through experience. He wrote, "God did not give us a spirit of timidity, but a spirit of power, of love, and of self-discipline" (2 Timothy 1:7, NIV).

Self-control is seen in a believer's life when all known evil and wrong is laid aside and excluded. Temperance does not imply that a moderate amount of a wrong is acceptable or that a moderate experiment with sinful practices is permitted. It is to bring everything in life in complete alignment with God's will. Temperance means moderation in all good things and total abstinence from all evil things. And it means even more. It means doing all possible good. It involves making the most of every talent, capacity, and opportunity in order that we become the best, most productive persons we have the potential to become.

It was customary in Paul's day to compare the Christian experience with athletes. To be a real athlete means to deny one's self everything that would possibly decrease one's best performance. It also means to actively pursue everything which will increase one's best skills. That seems so simple to talk about, but so difficult to implement. The secret is that the same spirit of determination and discipline asserted by the athlete must be devoted to Christ.

Self-control is gained when the goal of the believer is to glorify God, and not merely to desire the good of one's self or one's fellowman. *Self-mastery begins by yielding to the Great Master!*

There are many instances in Scripture of

what is included in self-control. The capacity for anger, the power of speech, the appetite for food, fun, and sex is involved. One's thoughts, temper, and money are all areas where the Holy Spirit expects commitment and control. All of these things are good and right under control and within the boundaries of God's will.

A small lad told his class at school that his fish all died during the night. When asked why, he replied that some water softener had gotten into their water and they all had softened to death. Many Christians have been softened to death by carelessness, ease, indifference, or just plain laziness — by lack of self-control.

Thus it should be noted that self-control and self-discipline are voluntary so far as one's commitment is concerned, but are borne out of a life that is first controlled by the Holy Spirit. Discipline is more than cold adherence to rules. It is sticking to a training program with a purpose beyond one's self. A disciple is one under discipline. A disciple submits to training and follows the road to attain the goal.

SUMMARY

As Christians we each are responsible to strive earnestly to become the best possible person, serving God and others at full potential. To enable us to attain this goal the Holy Spirit helps us to be faithful, meek, and disciplined. In bearing this kind of fruit we reflect the character of the Lord.

Faithfulness at all times, under all circumstances is a hallmark of true Christian character. Meekness is not weakness. Only those strong in the Lord can be truly meek. Only by self-control can we avoid all known evil and do all possible good.

These truths highlight the fact that in Christian living, being is of highest priority. But they also indicate that being thoroughly Christian results in worthy doing.

What Do You Think About These?

1. What do you understand faithfulness to mean? Give an example of faithfulness from the Bible; another from among your Christian acquaintances.

2. Is the author of this book correct in saying that meekness is not a sign of weakness, but rather of strength? Why do you answer as you do?

3. Explain what you understand by self-control.

4. Why is this triad of the Spirit's fruit so important in the making of a worthy character? Can there be true Christian character without any of them? Why?

If You Want to Dig a Little Deeper

1. How does 1 Samuel 30:24 relate to faithfulness?

2. Make a list of examples in Scripture and/or your own life experiences which illustrate how each of this triad of fruit has been evidenced in individuals.

3. Relate self-control to all the other elements of spiritual fruit.

Bible References Relating to This Chapter

[1]James 3:3.
[2]John 8:50.
[3]John 5:41.
[4]John 5:19, 30; 8:28.
[5]John 6:38.
[6]Galatians 6:1, 2 Timothy 2:24-25.

INTRODUCTION TO PART II

"Daddy, how can I believe in the Holy Spirit when I have never seen Him?" asked 12-year-old Jim. "I'll show you how," said the father.

He was an electrician, and so one day he took his young son to the power plant. There Jim saw the generators, and his father explained, "This is where the power comes from to heat our house and give us light. We cannot see the power, but it is in that machine and in the power lines." And he went on. "I know you believe in electricity, but you don't believe in it because you see it. You believe in it because you see what it can do. It is like that with the Holy Spirit. We do not believe in Him because we see Him, but we believe because we see what He does in people's lives."

The first section of this book has emphasized what the Holy Spirit does to transform, enhance, and empower the lives of men and women. We have seen that He, the Spirit of Christ, present and at work in the world, lives in the heart of every Christian. The Bible says, God sent the Spirit of His Son into our hearts. His presence brings to the believer Christlike attitudes and causes him to demonstrate those attitudes in his daily relationships toward God, with his fellowmen, and toward himself.

These Christlike virtues are in the Scriptures referred to as the fruit of the Spirit. Just as an apple tree bears apples, not pears, so every believer bears the Spirit's good fruit.

John Wesley refers to this Christian fruit as the "mind of Christ" and of it being essential to all believers. "Whoever hath not, is not of His," are Wesley's words. He goes on to say that the purpose of the Holy Spirit for Christians is "to fill them with 'love, joy, peace, long-suffering, gentleness, goodness, fidelity, meekness, and temperance;' to enable them to crucify the flesh, with the affections and lusts, its passions and desires; and in consequence of that inward change, to fulfill all outward righteousness; to 'walk as Christ walked' in 'the work of faith, in the patience of hope, and labour of love' (1 Thessalonians 1:3)."

While every Christian does indeed bear a full cluster of the Spirit's fruit, each one evidences that fruit in different ways and in varying measure in keeping with his own personality. And that fruitfulness increases in both quantity and quality as we cultivate the soil of our spirits and allow the grace of God more and more to control us.

The Christian is to be transformed by the

Holy Spirit, and then more and more be conformed to the image of Christ. The Apostle Paul wrote of this to the Corinthian believers. He said, "We, who with unveiled faces all reflect the Lord's glory, are being transformed into his likeness with ever-increasing glory, which comes from the Lord, who is the Spirit" (2 Corinthians 3:18, NIV).

It is, then, the fruit of the Spirit, displayed attractively in Christian lives, which reflects Christ's image and helps to convince other persons outside the kingdom of God of the reality and benefits of His salvation and so tends to draw them to the Lord.

The New Testament teaches that the Holy Spirit not only reflects Christ's likeness through fruitbearing believers, but that furthermore He gives particular gifts to each of those believers, thereby enabling them effectively to serve God and their fellowmen. We now enter into a consideration of those various gifts and their importance within the church and in the world around.

WHAT ARE SPIRITUAL GIFTS?

Relevant Scriptures: Acts 6:1-8, 10; 1 Corinthians 1:3-8; 12:1-7; Ephesians 4:1-7; Romans 12:3-8.

We have no record of Jesus ever referring to spiritual gifts. But the apostles Paul and Peter had considerable to say about them. These apostles, as Stanley D. Walters suggests, provide six different lists of such gifts: Romans 12:6-8; 1 Corinthians 12:8-11; 12:28; 12:29-31; Ephesians 4:11-12; 1 Peter 4:10-11.

What, really, are these gifts of which the apostles write? *Spiritual gifts are special abilities which God gives to believers in order that they may accomplish His work of grace among men.* Peter says, "Each one should use whatever gift he has received to serve others, faithfully administering God's grace in its various forms" (1 Peter 4:10, NIV). In fact, the Greek term most frequently translated "gifts" in the New Testament is *charismata,* the plural form of *charisma* which stems from *charis* meaning "grace." So it is that spiritual gifts are literally "grace gifts." The root meaning also includes joy and gladness — characteristics of the life so endued.

These enduements of God's grace through the spirit are essential to the effective growth and development of each believer, as well as for the outreach and edification of the church. Spiritual gifts help the church to function and to mature. They are not for observation, but for service to the glory of God.

Numerous helpful definitions of a spiritual gift have been given. Here are three:

1. "A special qualification granted by the Spirit to every believer to empower him to serve within the framework of the body of Christ."

2. "A divinely ordained spiritual ability through which Christ enables His church to execute its task on earth."

3. "An extraordinary endowment bestowed by the Holy Spirit sovereignly and undeservedly on believers as instruments for Christian service and church edification."

SPIRITUAL GIFTS AND NATURAL ABILITIES

The gifts of the Spirit must be distinguished from natural talents inherent in an individual's temperament or personality. There is, however, a close relationship between the spiritual gifts which God bestows and a person's natural talents or abilities. Spiritual gifts are neither identical to natural abilities and talents, nor are they totally different and unrelated. There are both similarities and differences.

Gifts, as well as talents and natural abilities, have their source in God. "What do you have that you did not receive?" (1 Corinthians 4:7, NIV). Both gifts and talents may be used for good or bad, for godly or selfish ends. They may produce the most beneficial or devastating results.[1] The quality and intensity of a gift or of a talent or an ability may vary from person to person.

Only Christians possess spiritual gifts, whereas most, if not all persons, including unbelievers, have natural abilities or talents which may be developed. Only those who possess the Holy Spirit can possibly claim the gifts of the Spirit.[2] The unbeliever does not and cannot have the gifts of the Spirit.[3]

Natural abilities and talents are given at our first birth. These the Holy Spirit may use for His purposes in the lives of believers, but in addition He also bestows spiritual gifts after a person is born again of the Spirit.

This is illustrated in the life of the Apostle Paul. Before his conversion he was a talented leader and persuader of men. But his gifts of healings, miracles, and apostleship were not given to him until after his conversion to Christianity.[4]

While talents and natural abilities come with the natural birth, spiritual gifts, although potentially present from the natural birth, are given with one's spiritual birth, or sometime thereafter.[5]

Another important distinction is that the unregenerated, natural man is dependent upon himself to discover, develop, and use his talent or ability. The believer, however, has the Holy Spirit to reveal what he possesses, to give discipline in the development of his capacities, and to empower him in using them.[6]

It may be impossible for human understanding to discern between a natural ability or a talent and a gift of the Spirit. If the person is a Christian, his special ability may be a gift of the Spirit. But if a person is not a Christian, the ability or talent is just that; it cannot be a spiritual gift. The Holy Spirit will reveal this to some Christians, at least, and sooner or later, all will know.

Comparative Lists of Spiritual Gifts

We have already noted that there is great diversity among the spiritual gifts. While most of them coincide and/or intersect at various points, each list or classification, as well as the interpretation of the separate gifts, is different enough to show difficulty to find unanimous agreement.

In our considerations here we shall first of all seek to show the diversity with evident congruency of the various categories; and then to give attention to the meaning and use of the diverse gifts of the Spirit.

David Brown categorizes the gifts enumerated by the Apostle Paul in 1 Corinthians 12 as follows:[7]

Pertaining to the intellect: the word of wisdom and the word of knowledge.

Dependent upon special faith: faith, healings, working of miracles, prophecy, discerning of spirits.

Referring to tongues: various kinds of tongues, interpretation of tongues.

Placed in their relative order of importance in 1 Corinthians 12:28-31, the same authorities believe there must be a distinction between and among the gifts, and in the manifestations and the operations of the Spirit as seen in the apostle's use of different terms. The further distinction is made that the gifts are the extraordinary powers conferred upon believers, who then have offices to fill where a special ministry is carried out in behalf of the whole body.

Dr. J. A. Huffman groups the overlapping expressions of 1 Corinthians 12:28-31 as follows:

● The offices or gifts of *instruction:* apostles,

prophets, teachers.

- The gifts of the *miraculous:* miracles, gifts of healing.
- The office of *relief and administration:* helps, governments.
- The gift of the *ecstatic:* kinds of tongues, the interpretation of kinds of tongues.

The contents of 1 Corinthians 13, is sometimes regarded as being an explanation of a gift of the Spirit, love. But more accurately, this is a fruit or grace of the Spirit. It is the result or work of God's Spirit in a person's inner being which issues in outward expressions, attitudes, and dispositions.

It seems important that clear distinction be made in the use of the terms mentioned above. A *ministry of the Holy Spirit* is first of all an expression of how the Holy Spirit relates to a believer. This could include, among other things, the filling of the Spirit, the anointing of the Spirit, the leading of the Spirit, the earnest of the Spirit, and the sealing of the Spirit. It also refers to a manner of working the Spirit has through a committed believer. It refers to a service rendered as assigned and abetted by the Holy Spirit.

On the other hand, the *office of a Christian believer* refers to the task or assignment itself, accompanied by the special spiritual gift bestowed to fulfill that assignment and to accomplish that service or ministry. The effects of the Spirit's gift to fulfill an office and to work a ministry may well be called a manifestation or evidence that the Holy Spirit is at work in that life. It is not as conclusive as a manifest fruit of the Spirit, but is nevertheless meaningful to a point.

APOSTOLIC LISTS OF THE GIFTS

God is a God of variety. This is seen not only in the natural world where the thousands of species and varieties are seen of both plants and animals, but also in the spiritual realm where the Spirit bestows a great variety of gifts to equip believers for service.

We noted earlier that in three separate epistles Paul lists spiritual gifts. These lists vary, although there is some overlapping. In addition to Paul's lists, we need to note Peter's. In some cases where offices or ministries, as defined and explained above, are used, the lists are given in uniform pattern to indicate the gift involved to fulfill the particular office.

Below, the lists of the apostles' are tabulated. The numbers in parentheses following the gifts in the Corinthians lists indicate the number of times the same gift is repeated in the lists given. The lists are:

Romans 12:3-8

1. Prophecy, v. 6
2. Serving (helps), v. 7
3. Teaching, v. 7
4. Exhorting, v. 8
5. Giving, v. 8
6. Leadership (ruling or government), v. 8
7. Showing mercy, v. 8

Ephesians 4:11

1. Apostleship
2. Prophecy
3. Evangelism
4. Pastoring
5. Teaching

1 Peter 4:10-11

1. Speaking, v. 11
2. Serving, v. 11

1 Corinthians 12:8-10, 28-30

1. Ability to speak with wisdom, v. 8
2. Ability to speak with knowledge, v. 8
3. Faith, v. 9
4. Healing, v. 9
5. Miracles, v. 10
6. Prophecy, v. 10 (3)
7. Discernment (ability to distinguish between spirits), v. 10
8. Tongues (ability to speak in other languages), v. 10
9. Interpretation (ability to interpret languages), v. 10
10. Apostleship, v. 28 (2)
11. Teaching, v. 28 (3)
12. Miracles, v. 28 (2)
13. Healing, v. 28 (2)
14. Serving (helps), v. 28 (3)
15. Leadership (ruling or government), v. 28 (2)
16. Tongues (ability to speak in other languages), v. 28 (2)

Prophecy, teaching, and serving are the only three gifts which appear three times in the various contexts, while apostleship, miracles, healing, leadership (ruling or government), and tongues (ability to speak in other languages) are used twice. What significance one may make of the repetition is a matter of pure conjecture, since there is no reference of the writers to the different lists in a comparative context.

There are other New Testament references where one could note additional descriptions or expressions of gifts, offices, or ministries. However, the lists above will be more than adequate to compare and contrast, identify and define in this study. The total of the gifts, then, in the lists given above, is no less than 21. Some of these may be dovetailed, since they seem to be overlapping, if not identical, even though different terms are used.

One of the evidences which has been suggested that these lists are not comprehensive or all-inclusive is that, just as the parts of the body are not all mentioned, so all the gifts of the body of Christ are not included. Since no two lists are exactly the same, it seems possible to conclude that no list could be all-inclusive, because the gifts of the Spirit are inexhaustible.

Still another widely held view is that every possible gift for believers in the body of Christ can be classified under one of the other gifts given in the apostles' lists. Thus, though not all are specifically mentioned, perhaps all other unnamed gifts can be categorized under one of those that is listed. Accordingly, each of the named gifts becomes an umbrella which covers a whole group of unrelated gifts.

As a case in point, Peter urges that believers should "offer hospitality to one another without grumbling. Each one should use whatever gift he has received to serve others, faithfully administering God's grace in its various forms" (1 Peter 4:9-10, NIV). It is readily apparent that hospitality may be classified under a larger category of serving or helps, which is mentioned three times in the above lists.

CLASSIFICATIONS OF THE GIFTS

Some of the many ways in categorizing the gifts include the following:

A. Since the idea of ministering saturates the function of the gifts, one method is to classify all of the gifts as ministering gifts with three subdivisions:

(1) *Speaking gifts* which include apostleship, prophecy, evangelism, pastoring, teaching, exhorting, word of wisdom, word of knowledge, tongues, and interpretation.

(2) *Serving gifts* or helps such as ministration or hospitality, giving, government or ruling, showing mercy, faith, discernment, miracles, and healing.

(3) *Signifying gifts* which include also miracles, healing, tongues, and interpreting tongues.

It is questionable whether the last division is necessary or even advisable, inasmuch as one of the errors against which Jesus warned seems to be intimated. It is that a wicked and adulterous generation seeks for a sign. The gifts are not given as signs or proofs of anything, even though at times they may demonstrate the power and ability of the Spirit as He works through open channels.

B. Another way of classifying the gifts is into three groups of three gifts, as follows:

(1) The gifts of *revelation* — the word of

wisdom, the word of knowledge, and the discerning spirits.

(2) The gifts of *powers* — the gift of faith, the gift of healing, and the working of miracles.

(3) The gifts of *utterance* — the gift of prophecy, the gift of tongues, and the gift of interpretation.

This method is quite interesting from the standpoint of the nine gifts enumerated in 1 Corinthians 12:8-10, but it has the weakness of discounting other expressions in the passages cited in this lesson.

C. A third method of classification utilizes only two categories, the service gifts and the language gifts:

(1) The *service gifts* — speaking for edification, exhortation, and comfort of others; service in ministering to human needs; teaching by grounding others in the truth; exhortation or encouragement whereby others are stimulated in faith; giving or sharing with generosity; compassion or concern; speaking with wisdom; the ability to grasp and communicate knowledge; faith as a mustard seed; gifts of healings; miracles as they are especially of grace; different kinds of languages; interpretation of languages; and discernment of spirits.

(2) The *language gifts* — speaking for edification, exhortation, and comfort for others; speaking with wisdom, different kinds of languages, and interpretation of languages.

It is obvious here that four of the gifts mentioned by Paul in 1 Corinthians 12 are simply lifted out of the service gift category for special notice and emphasis.

D. A fourth classification of the gifts divides the gifts into four categories as follows:

(1) The ministry of *helping* — serving, giving, showing mercy, craftsmanship, and healings.

(2) The ministry of *directing others* — leadership and faith.

(3) The ministry of *the Word* — gifts which have a direct relationship to the Word of God — apostleship, prophecy, evangelism, pastor-teacher, teaching, exhortation, wisdom, knowledge, discernment of spirits, and music.

(4) The ministry of *the spectacular* — miracles, tongues, and interpretation of tongues.

This general fourth division, adapted from Yohn's *Discover Your Spiritual Gift and Use It,* includes some things, such as music and craftsmanship, which may be regarded as skills or special abilities which are not included in the lists as based on the scriptures of this lesson.

E. A fifth method of classification uses only three divisions:

(1) The *enabling gifts* — apostleship, prophecy, evangelism, shepherding or pastoring, and teaching.

(2) The *serving gifts* — the word of wisdom, the word of knowledge, faith, gifts of heal-

ing, workings of miracles, discernment, helps and serving, administration and giving aid, exhortation, giving, and compassion.

(3) The *gifts of tongues,* and the interpretation of tongues.

F. A final method of classification, the one which will be used in the latter section of this book, is threefold:

(1) *The equipping gifts* — apostleship, prophecy, evangelism, pastoring, and teaching.

(2) *The gifts of utterance* — teaching, exhortation, preaching, languages, interpretation of languages.

(3) *The serving gifts* — wisdom, knowledge, faith, healing, miracles, discernment, helps, administration, giving, and showing mercy.

Although in this last grouping there is some overlapping, it is evident that strict categorization may not only be difficult but unnecessary to the full understanding of the Spirit's work in the believer. The fact that some spiritual gifts seem to shade into each other is illustrated by the gift of teaching. Evangelism must have some teaching content; prophecy incorporates some teaching; and pastoring or shepherding also involves teaching.

Some authorities urge that certain ones of the Spirit's gifts were intended primarily for the incubation period of the church, and therefore have disappeared today. There are, indeed, some qualifications of an apostle which cannot possibly be fulfilled literally today. For example, an apostle was to be one who had seen the Lord, and/or who was a witness of the resurrection of the Lord.

This example and argument is partially negated in that Paul did not literally see the Lord or witness His resurrection, as far as we know. But he did meet Christ on the road to Damascus in an unusual spiritual way. This was also after the Holy Spirit had been given at Pentecost, so we may conclude that "apostles" today may not mean what it did in the first century of the Christian era, but it still may have meaning so far as being ambassadors, emissaries, or missionaries is concerned. These offices, services, or ministries may still have special gifts of the Spirit which parallel with those in the early church.

Just as the New Testament apostles used other gifts, such as miracles and healing, to attest or authenticate their verbal ministry as from the Lord, so modern-day believers may expect to experience whatever endowment is necessary to effectively serve by the power, ability, and gifts of the Spirit.

For every need of the church, God has given adequate provision as administered by the Holy Spirit. Some examples of needs with the corresponding gifts that show respondence to meet that need are as follows:

- The need for preaching the Word — the gift

of prophecy.

- The need for instruction — the gift of teaching.
- The need for encouragement — the gift of exhortation.
- The need for help in difficulty — the gift of showing mercy.
- The need for financial support — the gift of giving.
- The need for vision for the future — the gift of faith.
- The need for protection — the gift of discernment.
- The need for reaching the lost — the gift of evangelism.

There can be no question as to the importance and use of spiritual gifts as seen in their purpose and function, even if there is no completely agreed-upon list or classification of the gifts. The task remains to interpret and try to understand the use which the Holy Spirit would make of each of the gifts through the believer's life. Later portions of the book give attention to this task.

SUMMARY

To understand the meaning and significance of spiritual gifts we must go to the teachings of the apostles — Paul and Peter in particular. Even they, however, do not identify the gifts exactly alike. This suggests that we can expect great variety among the gifts which the Spirit bestows upon the members of Christ's church.

From a consideration of the New Testament Greek term for gifts, we come to understand that spiritual gifts are actually "grace gifts" bestowed to assure maturation among the Christians and to empower them to reach out effectively into the world. Clearly, spiritual gifts are not given for show, but to enable God's people to serve other persons to His glory.

Seeking to categorize the gifts of the Spirit, Bible scholars provide a variety of lists. All provide a helpful base for study. But for the development of later sections of this book the author uses a threefold classification: the equipping gifts, the gifts of utterance, and the serving gifts.

Out of the most assuring truths which come from the study of the spiritual gifts is the fact that with every need and opportunity which comes to the Christian in his effort to build the kingdom of his Lord there is available to him through the Holy Spirit a corresponding, enabling gift of God's grace.

Gifts are not identical to talents. Gifts have to do with supernaturally bestowed abilities. Talents have to do with techniques and methods. Gifts depend upon spiritual endowments. Talents depend upon natural power. Gifts build up the saints, and something supernatural happens as the gift is exercised.

What Do You Think About These?
1. Where in the Bible do we turn for information about spiritual gifts?

2. What does the meaning of the Greek term for spiritual gifts indicate?

3. List differences and similarities between gifts and natural abilities.

If You Want to Dig a Little Deeper
Compare and contrast the several lists of the gifts provided by the author and other Bible students. Parallel these with those provided by the apostles. What facts seem evident from this exercise?

Bible References Relating to This Chapter
[1]Ephesians 4:15-16; 1 Corinthians 14:23.
[2]Romans 8:9, 14, 16-17; 1 Corinthians 12:7.
[3]1 Corinthians 14:16, 23-24.
[4]Acts 22:3-5; Galatians 1:15-16; Philippians 3:5.
[5]John 3:3-8.
[6]1Corinthians 2:4-5; Philippians 4:13; 2 Timothy 1:7.

Bibliography
[7]A Commentary on the Old and New Testaments by Robert Jamieson, A. R. Fausset, and David Brown, Volume VI, Grand Rapids, MI: Wm. B. Eerdmans, 1948.

THE GIVER IS GOD'S GIFT

Relevant Scriptures: John 14:15-21; 16:5-15; Acts 6:1-7; Romans 12:1-21; 1 Corinthians 1:4-9; 12:1-11; Ephesians 4:4-16.

In our concern with the fruit and gifts of the Spirit we must give due consideration to the Holy Spirit himself; for He it is who produces the fruit and bestows the gifts. He is God's great Gift to the church and to each individual member of the church.

It is He, not His benefits, we are supremely to cherish. It is He, not His gifts, we are to seek. When we have Him, we shall surely bear His fruit and share in His gifts. But only then.

The Holy Spirit is a person — the third person of the Divine Trinity. As surely as the Father and Son are persons, so is the Spirit. This is particularly evident at the time of Jesus' baptism. The Son is baptized of John, the Spirit descends upon Him, and the Father's voice is heard witnessing His approval.[1]

It is true that the Bible contains less about the Holy Spirit than about the Father and the Son. But He is actually the Author of the Bible; and as one writer points out, "His authorship there is occupied with the main and absorbing theme not of himself but of another person, the Son of God."

This is in keeping with what Jesus promised when He told His disciples about His departure from the earth and of the Spirit's coming to take His place to counsel, to help, and to stand by them. He said: "It is for your good that I am going away. Unless I go away, the Counselor will not come to you; but if I go, I will send him to you. . . . When he, the Spirit of truth comes, he will guide you into all truth. He will not speak on his own; he will speak only what he hears and he will tell you what is yet to come. He will bring glory to me by taking from what is mine and making it known to you" (John 16:7, 13-14 NIV).

Indicating further the work of the Holy Spirit, Jesus said He would reprove the world of sin, of righteousness, and of judgment.[2] It is the Spirit who reveals to men the glorious salvation God has provided in Jesus Christ, making clear His person and implementing His redeeming work in the hearts of all who repent and believe the gospel.

It is the Holy Spirit who draws people to Christ.[3] To be converted is to be born of the Spirit.[4] The Spirit witnesses to the new life in

Christ.[5] The Holy Spirit who regenerates us in conversion, making us new creatures in Christ, also subsequently sanctifies us wholly, cleansing the heart and filling us as we make Christ Lord.[6]

So it is that *the Giver is himself the Gift.* At any level of Christian experience spiritual fruit is borne, and the Spirit's gifts are given. But it is as we in obedience and faith allow Him full place in our hearts as sanctifying Lord that the fruit becomes more abundant and that we receive His gifts most freely.

The Holy Spirit, like the Father and the Son, has always been; and we see him at work in Old Testament times. He was the Agent of creation.[7] He is ever present in the created order.[8] He is mentioned in relation to human life.[9] The Holy Spirit strove with persons.[10] He gave special abilities, knowledge, and wisdom.[11] The Holy Spirit came upon judges and leaders to deliver the people of God from oppression and danger.[12] He related to men of God in moral and spiritual matters.[13] The Old Testament prophets told of a glorious coming day of the Spirit which we recognize as our own gospel dispensation initiated by the ministry of Jesus and the events of Pentecost.

All of these things testify to the fact that God's work of redemption and the impulses of response in the hearts of men are the province of the Spirit's ministry in all ages, before Pentecost and ever since that day.

In the light of all this, it is clear that in any consideration of the Spirit the most important factor is having the Spirit himself in our hearts. *The primary outward evidence of the Holy Spirit's presence is moral and ethical.* It is whether or not one is Christlike. "If anyone does not have the Spirit of Christ, he does not belong to Christ" (Romans 8:9, NIV).

THE BIBLICAL BASIS FOR GIFTS

One of the first explicit evidences that the Holy Spirit began early to distribute gifts of service to Christian believers is the case of the seven deacons chosen and dedicated to special tasks among the believers.[14] All seven were men of good reputation, whose characters were well known and accredited. Even more importantly they were filled with the Spirit.

All seven were also full of wisdom. Of Stephen it is said, ". . . he was a man full of faith and of the Holy Ghost." Here, then, are men to whom the Spirit had imparted gifts for service. Prudence, discretion, piety, economy, frugality, impartiality, and liberality — all of these qualities, it may be assumed, were present with the descriptions given of both the need and the qualifications for the task. The abilities or talents may have been present with these seven men from their natural birth, but now they were elevated to their highest good and usefulness in the church.

1 Corinthians 1:3-8 also indicates that believers such as those at Corinth had received various spiritual gifts. They were enriched or endowed and abounded in all utterance or in the ability to teach the doctrines of the faith Paul had in turn committed to them by the Holy Spirit.

Furthermore, the testimony of the gospel of Christ had wrought miracles among them. Every gift and every grace of God's Spirit was possessed by that church through its members. Some had one spiritual gift and others another, so they were as gifted as any body of believers to whom Paul ministered.

1 Corinthians 12:1-4 gives definite base for study of the gifts of the Spirit as well as do various passages in the Roman and Ephesian Epistles. 1 Corinthians 12:1 seems to indicate that the Corinthians had written to Paul about their spiritual gifts. There was also evident contention among these believers about their gifts, to which Paul responds that they should have understanding and knowledge.

The Holy Spirit never intended that there should be such divisions and schism in the body of believers as existed at the Corinth church. Gentiles in the congregation had known nothing but passionate and senseless worship, unguided as they had been without reason or truth.

Christ himself had shown the way to the Father through His promise of the Holy Spirit both by His miracles and by His teaching. Now all believers were to receive gracious endowments as well as the enduement of the Holy Spirit which would lead to the growth as well as the edification of the church. Accordingly, there were to be "diversities of gifts," "differences of administrations" and "diversities of operations" (1 Corinthians 12:4-6).

"Paul makes clear first, that *no one Christian is divinely endowed with all God's gifts.* Different gifts characterize different Christians. Second, he shows that all God's many spiritual gifts issue from the same Holy Spirit. He is the custodian and administrator of God's gifts." — Charles W. Carter

A final biblical base considered here is that found in Ephesians 4:1-7. From this text it is clear that God's purpose for His people corresponds to the prayer of Christ in John 17 for the unity of believers. The fruit of the Spirit is seen in lowliness and meekness, with patience, forbearance in love, and in an eagerness to maintain the bond of peace by means of the unity of the Spirit. There is further emphasis of this unity in such terms as "one body," "one Spirit," "one hope," "one Lord," "one faith," "one baptism," and "one God and Father of all."

Then Paul says that, "To each one of us grace has been given as Christ apportioned it. This is why it says: . . . (he) gave gifts to men" (Ephesians 4:7-8, NIV).

The biblical base for the gifts of the Spirit is seen here in the different offices and situations in the church for which special gifts and graces are imparted in accord with the mission of Christ. Each one receives a free gift according to the office or function the Spirit chooses for each, that the responsibility may be discharged according to His mind and will.

It should be reiterated that *every member of the body of Christ has been given a gift to carry out a specific task.* We are "one body in Christ, and every one members one of another" (Romans 12:5). Each member is important, and each member must function if the body is to be complete and healthy.

Spiritual gifts have various manifestations, varied ministries, and varieties of operation. Many Christians have wanted to impose a uniformity where God has laid down the principle of diversity. There are places where it is of utmost importance that there be unity. Paul, however, with regard to gifts, stresses over and over, diversity, diversity, diversity!

There are many gifts, many abilities, various ministries, but only one Spirit who disburses and bestows the gifts. In Him and His presence in the lives of the gifted comes the unity. When human gifts are given, the sincere giver desires to give something that is fitting and suited to the age, the needs, or the interest of the recipient. To every believer the Holy Spirit first of all gives himself, and then a gift, at least one to every person, and to some perhaps several.

The point of emphasis is not that each person has a variety and diversity of gifts, but that *the gifts vary from person to person; and that no gift is unimportant.*

How each gift is important is illustrated on an occasion when an eminent conductor held a rehearsal with an array of musicians in the orchestra and with a hundred-voice choir. At a wave of the baton the musicians with the choir followed the conductor over several bars of music, almost at full volume. Far back in the orchestra the oboe player decided to rest, thinking the din would cover his omission. Suddenly, in desperation, the conductor cried for the music to stop. "Where on earth is the oboe?" he shouted.

For the effectual function of the body of Christ and the harmony of His ministries and operations, each one must do his part. "For the body is not one member, but many" (1 Corinthians 12:14).

The New Testament speaks of those persons who had multiple gifts. Stephen has already been noted for his wisdom and faith, for his good reputation as a leader, teacher, and speaker. Philip had the gifts of wisdom, evangelism, and showing mercy. Two or more of the gifts may be in operation at the same time in a single person or with persons in unison.

Not only are gifts given in diversity but differing ministries are assigned. Each believer, in other words, will have a different combination of gifts and ministries. Each person will probably have a different arrangement of spiritual abilities and *ministries — outlets for service.* No two people, we believe, are exactly alike. Each one is unique and can do what no one else can do.

Without enumerating the various gifts, ministries, or operations of the Spirit in this context, it may be noted that it is the prerogative of the Holy Spirit to assign or appoint the gifts to each person according to His will. It is not our business to seek certain gifts. Divine dealing with individuals is pleasing to God, and believers have little difficulty recognizing that God's ways, like His thoughts, are higher than any human comprehension.

SUMMARY

The fruit and gifts of the Spirit are important in the lives of individuals and of the church. But we must ever keep in mind that we can have these only as we have the person of the Holy Spirit himself in our lives.

The Holy Spirit is God, as truly as are the Father and Son. He is in the world to reveal Jesus and to carry on His work among men. He has been involved in world affairs from the beginning, and we read of His activities in the Old Testament as well as in the New. But since His coming upon the early believers at Pentecost He has manifested himself more directly and intimately in the lives of God's people.

The New Testament teaches us a great deal about the functions of the Holy Spirit. Among those teachings is the fact that He has from the apostolic times until the present been giving gifts to Christian believers. These gifts supplement and enhance natural talents and capacities of Christ's followers so that they can effectively extend His kingdom throughout the world.

The Spirit's gifts differ among believers in that the tasks and needs of believers differ. But all gifts are important and imperative for the maturation and the expansion of the church.

What Do You Think About These?

1. What do you understand by the caption of this chapter: "The Giver Is God's Gift"?

2. What has been and is the function of the Holy Spirit in the world?

3. What four passages of the New Testament provide basic teaching about the gifts of the Holy Spirit?

If You Want to Dig a Little Deeper

What does the Bible teach about the work of the Holy Spirit in Old Testament times? Cite and discuss the teaching of at least five Old Testament passages which tell us about the Holy Spirit's work.

Bible References Relating to This Chapter
[1]Mark 1:9-11
[2]John 16:8
[3]John 6:44; Revelation 22:17
[4]John 3:5-8
[5]Romans 8:16-17
[6]1 Thessalonians 5:23-24
[7]Genesis 1:2; Psalm 33:6
[8]Psalm 139:7-10
[9]Job 27:3; Psalm 104:30
[10]Genesis 6:3
[11]Exodus 35:30; Judges 3:10
[12]Judges 6:34
[13]Psalm 5:11
[14]Acts 6:1-7

GIFTS ARE FOR A PURPOSE

Relevant Scriptures: Romans 1:8-12; 12:3-8; 1 Corinthians 12:8-18; Ephesians 4:11-16; 1 Timothy 4:12-16; 2 Timothy 1:6-11; 1 Peter 4:7-11.

Spiritual gifts are for use; not for admiration or for display. They are not personal ego-builders. The Spirit's gifts and God-given responsibilities go together. They must always be seen in the same context. Without a given responsibility a gift in any area would be useless. Without a gift to perform a certain responsibility the assignment to that responsibility would be an error.

The service principle involved in the gifts of the Spirit is clearly indicated in both Romans 12 and 1 Corinthians 12. In the former passage, verses 3-8, Paul shows that one's attitude toward self, toward rights and privileges, and toward capacities and responsibilities is crucial. The keys to this attitude for the Christian is humility toward self, cooperation with others, and stewardship of one's gifts and abilities.

The most obvious danger of many Christians is the temptation to overestimate their abilities, but it is just as much an error to underestimate one's gifts and spiritual endowments. The safeguard toward either extreme is to see that God has assigned to everyone a "measure of faith" (Romans 12:3).

In this same chapter (Romans 12) the apostle applies the analogy of the members of the physical body to the spiritual body of Christ. He shows that each Christian is to assume his share of responsibility in ministering to the needs of that spiritual body.

Though some of the gifts mentioned in Romans 12 may be more self-advertising than others and some more menial in their nature, all gifts are spiritual because they are prompted by the Holy Spirit and they are exercised by His power. Each gift carries its own limitations, and none of the gifts is to be neglected in order for ease, safety, or convenience.

It is evident also that all of them are practical and for the good of others. They also give honor, praise, and glory to God. *Not all of the gifts, however, are for use only within the body of believers.* Some of them definitely relate also to the world of the unredeemed.

Peter reinforces these points in his brief reference to spiritual enduements. "Each one should use whatever gifts he has received to serve others, faithfully administering God's grace in its various forms" (1 Peter 4:10, NIV).

Gifts, then, are not ends in themselves. Rather, they are means to the end that believers may effectively work together as a whole. "In each of us, the Spirit is manifested in one particular way, for some useful purpose" (1 Corinthians 12:7, NEB).

When gifts contribute to the total life of the believing community and when they extend the gospel to the world of unbelief for the redemptive purposes of God, one may be certain that the Holy Spirit is at work. But when the gifts are exploited for someone's own pleasure or glory, when they lead to suspicion and mistrust among Christians, danger signals need to be sounded.

THE FUNCTION OF SPIRITUAL GIFTS

Closely related to the purpose of the gifts is their function. The Holy Spirit's communication is two directional. It benefits the believer in a spiritual way. Like everyone else to whom the Spirit manifests himself through the believer, that person himself is edified and benefited. In short, all of God's blessings are for all of His people in varying measure.

Paul also makes it clear that the Spirit's function is to illumine, purify, and enliven the believer's natural mental powers.

We observed earlier that the ultimate work

of the Holy Spirit is to testify of Christ and to glorify Him with the Father. Christ is glorified when His Person is lifted up, when His purposes are served and His will accomplished. The Holy Spirit works to bring each of us to Christ, to bring Christ to us, and through us to bring others to Christ.

Spiritual gifts exercised apart from that principle miss their mark and tend to cause confusion, squabbling, or unhealthy self-advertisement. On the other hand, if one attempts to serve without divine enabling, there will be little of lasting value or influence. The function of spiritual gifts is not to prove or exhibit anything. It is to serve others and to glorify God. Self-gratification or self-glorification are out of divine order.

Spiritual gifts must continuously be consecrated to God. Human organization and planning are important and human resources are needed to carry on the Lord's work, but all of these things are inadequate in themselves. To minister to the needs of modern man there must be the dynamic of the Holy Spirit. Nothing less than the supernatural resources of God will equip the church and its members to meet the challenges of this generation.

When the function of the gifts is not realized to the full, it probably is because of neglect. This could be based on ignorance, indifference, or lethargy concerning God's equipment, provision, or work in one's life. Or it could be an unwillingness to respond to some service assignment. *Neglect of the spiritual gifts will stifle personal growth and cripple the outreach of the church.*

We have already seen that the spiritual gifts function in the context of natural abilities. God does not allow our natural abilities to go to waste. In some cases, as has been noted, the Holy Spirit, by His gifts, may heighten one's natural abilities, but at other times they may function independently of or in addition to natural aptitudes. In any case, all the gifts of the Spirit as dispersed variously to each believer will complement and blend harmoniously with human talents in the body of Christ.

Although it is possible that a spiritual gift may operate in a person's life without his knowledge, understanding the function of that gift is most beneficial. It gives that person opportunity to cooperate more fully with God, as well as to work with others in the overall task of the church. As the gifts and workings of the Spirit are understood in the lives of others, there will be a greater sense of fulfillment of God's purpose and the stream of His activity through the body of believers.

DISTRIBUTION OF SPIRITUAL GIFTS

The Apostle Paul states in 1 Corinthians 12,

several principles which govern the distribution of spiritual gifts. First they are of great value. Understanding the full measure of their benefit, in human terms, may never be possible. But a gift's measure must be in terms of the degree to which it serves the interest and needs of the whole church.[1]

Some Christians may be tempted to claim special value to himself for one or more of the gifts, but that is not the teaching of Paul. Each spiritual gift, as well as all of them, are for the good of the whole body; specifically to build up the believers in the body of Christ. All gifts would, therefore, be important. "To each one is given the manifestation of the Spirit for the common good" (1 Corinthians 12:7, NASB).

The order prevailing in listing the gifts suggests, however, that they are not all of equal importance. This fact is suggested in that there are numerous gifts which are listed repeatedly in the New Testament. When placed together they make an imposing list.

It would appear that such gifts are of greater significance than others mentioned only once. Added to this is the fact that Paul ranks them himself as "first apostles, second prophets, third teachers . . ." (1 Corinthians 12:28, NASB).

Further, we note that some of the gifts are rigidly regulated while others are not.[2] The conclusion must be, therefore, that *some gifts are so* very practical and useful that to regulate or place boundaries on them would be superfluous and unnecessary. It is also clear that no gift whatever can compare with the fruit of the Spirit which is basically love in all of its various ramifications. No gift is to be used apart from the fruit of love.

Another principle which may be noted is that *different gifts are given to different people by the sovereign will of God alone.*[3] The gifts, as previously stated, are related in every case to the need of the body of Christ and the responsibilities placed on each individual. No Christian has all of the gifts. Every Christian has at least one. Christians do not all have the same gift.

A final principle of the distribution of the gifts is that *the variety of spiritual gifts should unify rather than divide the church.*[4] To make this point Paul applies the analogy of the physical body to the spiritual members of Christ's family. God does all of the arrangements for His purposes, whether in the physical or the spiritual realm.

RECEIVING SPIRITUAL GIFTS

Spiritual gifts are never given as a reward or compensation for service. *The gifts cannot be obtained by human effort.* It is presumptive for a person to specify which gift or gifts the Spirit should grant him. The gifts are given as the Spirit wills.

115

Any person who asks for a particular gift, function, or place in the service of Christ is out of order. This is illustrated in the request of James and John. They asked that Jesus grant them special places in His kingdom.[5] Although the subject of spiritual gifts is not specifically involved in this instance, the point that Jesus makes is the same. There are some things in the life of the Spirit that simply do not come by human manipulation or personal whim.

Nor is there any way that a person may come by a certain gift through training, study, or the learning of some mechanical or mystical formula. How to perform miracles or do spectacular deeds cannot be taught; nor can one who has a special gift coach another person how to perform the act for which he is gifted.

No one has the ability of the authoritative appointment to help the Holy Spirit distribute the gifts in the church. He is fully able and willing to make His will and way known to those who are open to receive what He has to give.

A person who has a natural skill or has developed an ability to perform an apparent miracle can be sure that he has something other than a spiritual gift. It may be something psychological or mystical, or physical, but it is not a gift of the Spirit. It may even be something of demonical nature. One needs to see clearly that to tamper with spiritual things by human manipulation is dangerous.

116

Of the many instances in Scripture of spiritual gifts being received and used there is not a single case where a person received such a gift because he asked for or sought it in prayer. Nor is there evidence that when a person received a spiritual gift from the Holy Spirit that he had the power to turn it off and on at will or use it when and how he wished.

It is evident that the person through whom the Holy Spirit was pleased to operate was open, committed, and filled with the Spirit. In the Corinthian church, this was not the case; therefore, Paul had to give special instruction about how the gifts were to be received and exercised.

There are two scriptures which seem to suggest an apostle could bestow a gift. Follow closely as we study these.

When the Apostle Paul contemplated a trip to Rome and a visit among the believers there, he stated that his longing was stimulated by more than a desire for personal gratification. He was concerned for their needs. Then he states the specific concern he had: "That I may impart to you some spiritual gift to make you strong — that is, that you and I may be mutually encouraged by each other's faith" (Romans 1:11-12, NIV).

The question here, of course, is whether Paul had the power or authority to impart a spiritual gift. The word *charisma,* which is used here, does denote the extraordinary gifts of the Spirit in quite a few passages of the New Testament. Some authorities suggest that it may here imply the special sanctifying work of the Holy Spirit as performed at Pentecost.

In other scriptures there is also a suggestion that the apostles were eager to equip new believers with this gift.[6] The purpose of Paul's "spiritual gift" was so they would be established or strengthened in the Lord.

Paul may be using "gift of grace" in Romans 1:11 in an ordinary sense with reference to salvation and eternal life.[7] In other instances he uses the expression "gift of grace" to denote extraordinary powers bestowed upon individuals by the Holy Spirit. In his letters to Timothy, Paul uses the expression with reference to "the sum of the powers requisite for the discharge of the office of an evangelist" (Vincent).[8]

"It seems that the apostle would be concerned to share with them some spiritual grace that would help to establish the Roman believers in their Christian experience. We cannot see how a miraculous gift would do this, except the gift of the Holy Spirit himself. To us it seems most reasonable to hold that Paul was talking about a further gift of God's grace, 'to the end ye may be established.' This fits in with the basic meaning of the term." — Ralph Earle

Whatever the meaning of this passage, the **result to both Paul and the Roman Christians** would be a strengthening in the Lord for service. It is quite contrary to other passages of Scripture given through the Apostle Paul to conclude that any person, even an apostle, had the power or authority to give the gifts of the Spirit in the extraordinary sense to others.

Further observations with reference to receiving the gifts of the Spirit need to be made on the basis of Paul's exhortations to Timothy: "Do not neglect the gift, which was given you through a prophetic message when the body of elders laid their hands on you" (1 Timothy 4:14, NIV).

It is utterly impossible from this scripture to conclude that the spiritual gifts are distributed by human means with the act of laying on hands, or that humans will be given the ability to predict how the Spirit will operate in anyone's life. Timothy was endowed by the Holy Spirit for the work of exhortation and teaching. He was a minister of the gospel; and when set aside for this purpose by the imposition of hands, the Holy Spirit gave Timothy the gift or gifts needed to perform the ministry to which the Spirit had appointed him. The gift was directly imparted by the Holy Spirit.

As for the prophetic involvement, it is most reasonable to conclude that when Paul visited Lystra on his first missionary journey and when he led Timothy to a personal faith in Christ, he may have perceived that here was a special vessel of the Lord who would be used in advancing the gospel. The Lord, after all, communicated with Ananias at Damascus that Saul was a "chosen vessel." But this is altogether apart from any concept that the apostles were empowered to set workers aside and decide what gifts they would have for the ministries they were to assume.

"Each God-called minister is equipped by the Holy Spirit with the necessary gift for fulfilling his solemn duties in preaching the word of God. *The gift is from God as a part of one's preparation for the work of the ministry; but its improvement and enlargement is man's responsibility.* God calls a minister, the Spirit equips him by His indwelling presence and the bestowal of spiritual gifts. The church ordains him by impressive ceremonies befitting such a call."—Roy S. Nicholson

It is obvious from Paul's word to Timothy that what he receives may be substantiated by others who are filled with the Spirit, and that their blessing and encouragement may be added. But that it is ultimately God's business to equip His servants for what He wills them to do.

The primary gift which Timothy had received was the Holy Spirit himself. But in addition Timothy was endowed with the necessary abilities to do the work to which God had called him. This idea permeates the epistle of Paul to Timothy. God gives the gifts to serve, but they are developed as exercised in an atmosphere of humility, faith, and dependence upon the Spirit who has given them.

USING SPIRITUAL GIFTS

There is every evidence in the New Testament that the Holy Spirit exercises His ministry when and how He pleases, through the lives of committed believers. The very idea of surrender and commitment includes the idea of being used as the Holy Spirit directs.

Only the Holy Spirit knows the time, place, and manner in which His gift or gifts will most glorify God and best serve His purpose. In the Book of Acts there are numerous instances where the Holy Spirit willed the exercise of a gift, and then at other times when He did not will such exercise. The gift of healing was exercised[9], but when there was no further need it was no longer exercised. Other examples include the gift of prophecy[10], the gift of miracles[11], and the gift of discernment[12].

Likewise the gift of unlearned languages was for the purpose of evangelistic communication. Although it is a question as to whether the miracle which occurred on the day of Pentecost as described in Acts 2, was in the ability that the apostles were given to speak in unlearned languages or whether it was a miracle which occurred in the hearing ear of the Pentecostal visitors, it would appear most reasonable to conclude that it was an ability or a gift which was given the apostles themselves. After all, they were the real believers; they were the channels the Spirit chose to use in the communication of truth. They were also the ones to whom the Holy Spirit with all of His presence and power had been immediately promised by Christ. This conclusion seems compatible with other instances where the apostles spoke in unlearned languages.

The only other instances in Acts where the gift of unlearned languages was used were at the house of Cornelius[13] and at Ephesus.[14] In each case varied language groups were present.

Since the gifts are bestowed upon believers as the Holy Spirit pleases, including when and where,[15] no person can exercise a particular gift any time and place he chooses. No matter how saintly or how long a person may have experienced the Spirit-filled life, no believer is so wise and so spiritually minded that he can decide when, how, and where to exercise a gift. It is only as the Holy Spirit leads that this is possible.

If true gifts in these areas are to be exercised, a person cannot perform miracles or speak in unlearned languages whenever he chooses or when he prays that he might do so. The gifts are not given to a person to possess. God bestows the gifts, but they still belong to Him. He retains sovereignty over them.

A prophet, one who speaks forth the truth, whether it concerns the present or the future, exercises the gift of prophecy only when he is "borne along" by the Spirit to do so (2 Peter 1:21). It is the Holy Spirit who impels men.

One who is given the power to exercise faith for healing on one occasion will not necessarily have the same ability on every occasion, or even on any other occasion. The gift of healing cannot be called forth by the recipient at his own beck and call.

Another fact is that the exercise or use of a gift on different occasions does not imply that it gets easier to use the gift as it is exercised. The development or enlargement of a gift does not mean in human terms that it becomes easier to use, and therefore, will be used more frequently. What it does mean is that the Holy Spirit through the believer has continual and increasing control, freedom, and bestowal of His will for service to the body of believers.

The Apostle Paul had the gift of healing.[16] But he could exercise this gift only upon occasions when the Holy Spirit was willing for him to do so.

Other instances show that Paul himself was handicapped with some physical, mental, emotional, or social thorn in the flesh. Timothy was rather weak and sickly, together with another of Paul's co-workers whom he left "sick at Miletus."[17]

We may conclude rather categorically that a person will have the free use of his will as long as he lives, as he remains yielded to the Spirit's control. However, a person can choose not to use a spiritual gift which the Holy Spirit has bestowed. He may neglect the gift.[18] In neglecting a gift a person may very well lose it and he may thereby grieve the Holy Spirit.[19]

A believer's free will can also be exercised in the desire and purpose to fulfill all the will of God. In this case the attitude of obedience gives the Holy Spirit freedom to use His chosen vessel to the glory of the Father and to the good of other persons. But no person has sovereignty over the Holy Spirit in the use and exercise of the spiritual gifts.

A person who can, at his own will, call up a gift and exercise a gift to the point where it becomes more and more for his own purposes and desires may have a human psychological phenomenon for display. But that is not a gift of the Spirit. It could even be a work of Satan to deceive the unsuspecting and undiscerning believer.

SUMMARY

The Holy Spirit grants His gifts to believers to enable them effectively to reach men for Christ and to build them up in the faith. To seek to use spiritual gifts for other purposes is to exploit them.

These important gifts are distributed freely among all of the believers in accordance with the service to which God appoints these persons. While some gifts are more significant than others, all are important, actually essential, in doing God's work in the world. Even the least gift is to be cherished and exercised.

Gifts of the Spirit must be received as the Spirit in His sovereignty distributes them, and they must be used only under His direction, for the glory of God.

What Do You Think About These?
1. Why does the Holy Spirit grant special gifts to Christians?
2. What are some of the principles which determine how spiritual gifts are distributed?
3. What should be the believer's attitude toward the gifts he receives?
4. What is to determine when and how our special gifts are used?

If You Want to Dig a Little Deeper
Having answered the above questions, cite at least one scripture passage relevant to each of your answers.

Bible References Relating to This Chapter
[1] 1 Corinthians 12:7; 14:6, 19
[2] 1 Corinthians 14:27-28
[3] Romans 12:6; 1 Corinthians 12:11-18; 28-30

[4]1 Corinthians 12:14ff.
[5]Mark 10:37-38
[6]Acts 8:16-17; 10:44-45; 19:1-6; 1 Thessalonians 3:2
[7]Romans 5:15-16; 6:23
[8]1 Timothy 4:14; 2 Timothy 1:6
[9]Acts 5:16; 8:7; 9:18, 34; 14:10
[10]Acts 5:9; 15:32; 20:25, 29; 21:4, 9, 11
[11]Acts 6:8; 8:6, 13; 9:40; 13:11; 16:18; 19:11
[12]Acts 5:3; 14:9
[13]Acts 10:46; 11:15; 15:8
[14]Acts 19:6
[15]1 Corinthians 12:11
[16]Acts 14:8-11
[17]2 Corinthians 12:7-10; 1 Timothy 5:23; 2 Timothy 4:20
[18]1 Corinthians 14:32
[19]Ephesians 4:30

THE EQUIPPING GIFTS

Relevant Scriptures: Romans 12:3-8; 1 Corinthians 12:8-10, 28-30; Ephesians 4:11; 1 Peter 4:10-11.

In any group of genuine Christian believers there is a great deal of spiritual life and energy, and any number of spiritual gifts are present. Some of that energy and those gifts may, however, for several reasons be quite unproductive in kingdom building. The Apostle Paul suggests the likelihood of such a situation in an admonition to one of his younger and somewhat timid co-workers. He wrote to Timothy: "I remind you to fan into flame the gift of God, which is in you . . . for God did not give us a spirit of timidity, but a spirit of power, of love and of self-discipline. So do not be ashamed to testify about our Lord" (2 Timothy 1:6-8, NIV).

In order to help fire that smoldering energy, in order to instruct and direct the spiritual life in any Christian group, God has placed persons with special gifts. The exercise of those gifts equips the believers to do God's work in the world with greater effectiveness. We are now going to consider some of those gifts.

The equipping gifts are mentioned as offices in the church at Ephesus. We shall look at them here as they relate also to other New Testament groups. They have also been referred to as the "enabling gifts" because they are associated with "the officers of the church, whose task it is to enable the Christian community to serve and to minister." They may be regarded as being among the most basic and significant, since they equip leaders and other believers in the church to build up and prepare the body of Christ for ministry and service.

APOSTLESHIP

Ephesians 4:11; 1 Corinthians 12:28

In both of these passages the work of an apostle stands first. The apostles had distinguishing features, such as: a commission directly from Christ, a witness of the Resurrection, special inspiration, supreme authority, accreditation by miracles, and unlimited commission to preach and to establish churches.

The word "apostle" means "sent on a mission with a commission." It is used at least 75 times in 19 of the 27 books of the New Testament. One of the stock questions with regard to the gift of apostleship is: Does it still exist or did it cease with the first-century church?

Apostleship is often thought of in the sense that an apostle must have been among those persons who had been with Jesus in His human experience, who had received a personal call and commission from Christ,[1] who had witnessed the Resurrection, who laid the doctrinal foundation of the church,[2] who had power to perform miracles, who laid the structural foundation of the church, and who will someday sit on 12 thrones judging the 12 tribes of Israel with their names inscribed on the 12 foundations of the New Jerusalem.[3] If that is the only meaning of the term *apostle,* it is true then that no succeeding generation has ever met or can meet the necessary qualifications.

If, however, the term *apostle* is used other than in this restricted sense, in a broader context, it includes also such men as Barnabas;[4] James, the Lord's brother;[5] Silas and Timothy;[6] and Andronicus with Junia.[7] There is an evident shift to the broader, itinerant, missionary ministry of establishing congregations of believers in regions beyond. Perhaps a working definition with relevant meaning and application today is, *"The apostle is one who is sent to minister transculturally with church-planting goals."* Such a person would also be one who would never be undisturbed by the thud of heathen feet on the road to eternity without God.

It is safe to conclude that the gift of apostleship, at least in its unrestricted, narrow sense, is given today for the extension, nurture, and instruction of the church. This is not to hold the idea that there is an apostolic succession with some kind of automatic transfer of authority by ritualistic or mechanical means. Apostleship is not parallel with that of a pastoral function. The pastor is one who ministers to a single congregation for a period of time. Apostleship is that mission to non-Christian areas for the purpose of transplanting the Christian faith — a missionary. To the office of the apostle, the Holy Spirit communicates a gift or perhaps several gifts to fulfill the ministry.

PROPHECY

Romans 12:6; 1 Corinthians 12:10; Ephesians 4:11

The term "prophecy" may immediately suggest the predicting or foretelling of future events. It can and does mean this in some instances. But it is much more. Paul defines it as being a means of strengthening, encouraging, and comforting the believers.[8]

The basic meaning of the word is "to speak," so that one who proclaims or interprets a message from God may have the needed gift to do so. It is a characteristic gift of those who preach the gospel, and Peter states that to speak the very words of God is a spiritual gift (1 Peter 4:10-11).

Paul shows the importance of this gift as an endowment when he urges that prophecy is to be preferred far above speaking in unfamiliar languages which can be understood by no one.[9] *This gift is primarily for the edification of the church, although there may be exceptions where unbelievers are also convinced.*

Just as with the other gifts of the Spirit, there may be a counterfeit as well as the genuine. Christ warned against "false prophets," especially in the last days.[10] The warning was repeated by most of the other writers of the New Testament as well.[11]

The church is equipped with some very objective checks with regard to the veracity of this gift. With the Word of God as the objective standard of evaluation and the Holy Spirit witnessing internally to discerning hearts, one does not need to suffer from delusion and error.[12] No believer will identify this gift with that of extrasensory perception, with fortune-telling, with the horoscope, or with astrology.

Like the gift of apostleship, prophecy may take on a different form in our age than it did in New Testament times. Insofar as a continuing written revelation is concerned, which was one of the functions of the Bible prophets, that element does not have relevance today. The gift of prophecy may be experienced and demonstrated in both oral utterance, such as preaching, when a person has faithfully studied the Word of God and then stands to declare its unsearchable riches; or it may be a gift which is also available for writing the words of truth, where fresh insights and spiritual encouragement come to both writer and reader.[13]

A working definition of prophecy is "the Spirit-given ability to proclaim, declare, or express in writing the message and meaning of the Word of God with clarity and to apply it to relevant, current situations with the effect of edifying, encouraging, or consoling believers."

EVANGELISM

Ephesians 4:11

Although the word for "evangelist" occurs only two other places in the New Testament,[14] John Wesley regarded the office of the evangelist, as being one of the extraordinary gifts, along with those of apostleship and prophecy.

There seems to be evidence in the New Testament that this office and its accompanying gift of apostleship was especially fitted for moving from place to place with the message of salvation, all the while being unfettered from the details of discipline, ritual, or organization. In this sense it may have been an auxiliary function of an apostle who was vitally involved in organizing and training believers.[15]

The work of evangelism precedes that of a pastor and a teacher. Its primary purpose is that of reaching the unsaved. The message is the good news of salvation, the gospel of Jesus Christ. The gift exercised in the Holy Spirit results in decisions among unbelievers. The itinerant ministry, where this gift would most commonly be exercised, is not for the primary purpose of building up the saints. This may also result, but it would be secondary to the ultimate goal.

That this gift may be in wide use today is illustrated in the proliferation of ways in which current innovation has resulted in the salvation of thousands:

> Beach evangelism
> Bible distribution
> Camp meetings
> Campus evangelism
> Child evangelism
> Coffeehouse evangelism
> Door-to-door evangelism
> Friendship evangelism
> High school Bible clubs
> Home Bible studies
> Hospital evangelism
> Jews for Jesus movement
> Literature evangelism
> Open-air evangelism
> Prison evangelism
> Radio and TV evangelism
> Rescue mission evangelism

Servicemen's evangelism
Street-corner evangelism
Writing of books, letters, tracts

Although each of the above are primarily methods or opportunities for evangelism which believers are taking advantage of, some of the methods call for considerable expertise which cannot be completely explained on the basis of training, talents, or skills. They are means which the Spirit uses and for which He gives extraordinary spiritual gifts.

A working definition is that *evangelism is a spiritual gift given to "proclaim the good news of salvation so effectively that unbelievers respond to the claims of Christ in conversion and commitment to Christian service."*

PASTORING

Ephesians 4:11

This gift is mentioned only in the Ephesian letter. *The word "pastor" comes from a Greek term which means shepherd.* It carries the idea of one who cares for sheep, with corresponding emphases on protection, concern, discipline, personal attention, self-sacrifice, and the sense of responsibility for both the flock and individual sheep as well.

This gift provides understanding and sensitivity for people and their needs. It need not be limited to or confined within a vocational context. *Many laymen, as well as the ordained clergy, may have this gift,* although in the former it may be utilized in a different manner.

The Greek terms in the New Testament are rather interchangeable in their usage. All of them refer to pastoring or shepherding. One means an overseer and in the King James Version is translated *bishop.* The second term means one who has the oversight or leadership of believers, and implies that by reason of age or spiritual maturity, this person is entrusted with a responsibility and exercises a gift. The third (shepherd) we noted in an earlier paragraph.

The pastor is not appointed by man, although others may lay hands on his head in ordination. He is a person with a divine appointment and a call to shepherd God's people. *The pastor's primary task is to feed and nourish, to guide and to serve.* He is called to equip and to enable the body of Christ for life in the world.[16]

It seems irrefutable that "pastor" should be considered synonymous with "elder" or "bishop" in the New Testament. A Sunday school teacher, for example, may have some of the shepherding gifts. His work with the members of his class may be as significant as that of any pastor to the same group.

Every pastor should welcome the service of laymen in helping to shepherd God's people. The pastor will recognize "under shepherds" who are able to extend his own ministry many times.

The word "pastor" suggests a pastoral scene such as given in Psalm 23, where the shepherd gently leads and guides the flock to nourishment and refreshment. Isaiah 40:11 also gives a beautiful portrait of the shepherd. Like the shepherd, a true pastor will guard as well as guide the flock. He knows how to use the rod as well as the staff, but always in loving concern.

The New Testament shows that a pastor must have certain qualifications.[17] He is to be hospitable, a lover of goodness, a master of himself, holy, upright, not quick-tempered or arrogant — in short, blameless.

The pastor is not to "lord it over" the flock but to serve the sheep. If the people of God are to be served, they must be led, not driven. He is a shepherd, not a cowboy. The pastor is not a dictator. He sacrifices himself for the sake of the flock.

Among the highest of God's spiritual gifts to the church are those entrusted to pastors. Exercised through the dedicated life of an ordained pastor, these gifts will be used by the Spirit so that Christians will mature in Christ under such sanctified care.

Some Christian communities have set up shepherding or discipling plans for the express purpose of bringing young believers into a more mature life in Christ. Every new Christian is assigned to an older, more mature believer who calls upon him if he is absent from public worship; encourages him in prayer and Bible study; guards him against false teachers or teachings; and, in general, exercises tender loving care toward him.

TEACHING

Romans 12:7; Ephesians 4:11; 1 Corinthians 12:28

Some authorities believe the office of the pastor and the teacher are inseparable. One authority states that "the omission of the article from teachers seems to indicate that pastors and teachers are included under one class." He further remarks that no man is fit to be a pastor if he cannot teach, and the teacher also needs the knowledge that pastoral experience gives. They would call this gift "pastor-teacher."

The context of 1 Corinthians 12:28 does not so specifically connect the two offices or functions. Here it would seem that a teacher is to instruct believers in the principles of truth, the elements of the Christian faith, and in their duties to each other.

Therefore, whether seen in close relationship to the work of a pastor or more unique in its arena of operation, *the gift of teaching is an enabling or equipping gift for the purpose of systematically imparting truth in a relevant way so that the gospel may be applied to the real world.*

The teacher makes truth live for others because it lives in him.

Among the last words of Christ to His disciples was His commission to teach all nations to observe all that He had commanded His disciples.[18] In order to maintain proper spiritual growth and health, believers require sound teaching.

Paul with Peter and others continued to teach under some of the most adverse circumstances, recognizing its importance as well as their gifts in this area. For the purpose of teaching the believers, Paul spent a whole year at Antioch, eighteen months at Corinth, with a two-year stay at Ephesus.[19] Both James and Peter in their letters to believers urged the importance of sound teaching as well as of warning against false teachers.[20]

Through the exercise of the gift of teaching, unity and strength are developed among believers. Teaching provides the body of Christ with understanding, so that believers have the opportunity and privilege of growing into maturity.

SUMMARY

To enable the church to serve the purposes of God in this present world, the Holy Spirit endows leaders in each generation with equipping gifts.

These equipping or enabling gifts are in the New Testament referred to as: apostleship, prophecy, evangelism, pastoring, and teaching.

Apostleship had particular significance in relation to the Twelve whom Jesus chose as His special helpers and representatives. The gift seems originally to have been given to men who had personally been with Jesus and received His direct call. They had been eyewitnesses of the Resurrection, had been given special powers to work miracles as well as special insight and authority to establish and direct the affairs of Christ's early church.

The term, however, even in New Testament times, came to have a broader application and was used in reference to several of the first-century churchmen who had not been with Jesus during His life on earth — such men as Paul, Barnabas, Silas, and Timothy. Today this gift seems to be given to persons whom God has appointed to extend, nurture, and instruct the church worldwide.

The spiritual gift of *prophecy* is to equip leaders to proclaim, interpret, and apply the truth of God. That truth may involve foretelling future events and it may not. Always, even in Old Testament times, the major work of the prophet was to declare God's eternal truth, whatever its implication might be.

The gift of *evangelism* equips a person to proclaim the gospel particularly to the unsaved in an appealing, convincing, and convicting manner.

Pastoring, on the other hand is a gift equipping the person to serve as a loving, diligent shepherd and overseer to the body of the believers.

Closely related to the work of the pastor is that of the *teacher.* The teaching gift may, in fact, be a part of the pastor's equipment. By this the recipient is enabled to impart God's truth in a practical, direct, and winsome manner making it relevant to the one being taught and encouraging him to apply it to his life.

What Do You Think About These?
1. What are the equipping gifts?
2. Describe the purpose of each.

If You Want to Dig a Little Deeper
1. Having listed and described the several equipping gifts, illustrate each of them from scripture.

Bible References Relating to This Chapter
[1]Mark 3:14; John 20:21
[2]Acts 2:38-41; 8:14-17; 10:44-48; Ephesians 2:20
[3]Luke 22:29-30; Revelation 21:14
[4]Acts 14:4, 14
[5]Galatians 1:19
[6]1 Thessalonians 1:1; 2:6-7
[7]Romans 16:7

[8] 1 Corinthians 14:3
[9] 1 Corinthians 14:1; 22-25
[10] Matthew 7:15; 24:11, 24
[11] 2 Peter 2:1; 1 John 4:2
[12] Deuteronomy 18:21-22; 1 John 4:1
[13] 1 Corinthians 14:3
[14] Acts 21:8; 2 Timothy 4:5
[15] 1 Corinthians 4:17; 16:10; 3 John 3, 5-8
[16] 1 Peter 5:2-3
[17] Titus 1:7-9
[18] Matthew 28:19-20
[19] Acts 11:26; 18:11; 19:10
[20] James 3:1; 2 Peter 2:1

THE GIFTS OF UTTERANCE

Relevant Scriptures: Romans 12:3-8; 1 Corinthians 12:8-10, 28-30; 14:1-40.

Among all of earth's creatures only man has the ability to speak. Only he can verbally express his deepest emotions and his greatest ideas. This amazing faculty is one of the most important building blocks of civilization. It is said that over 75 percent of the communication between one person and another is by word of mouth.

This ability to speak can be both a blessing and a bane, depending on what is being communicated. Years ago Henry Thoreau expressed this well. He had strolled over from Walden Pond and saw workmen connecting the first telephone lines from Texas to Maine. Someone said to him, "Mr. Thoreau isn't it wonderful that the people of Maine will be able to speak to the people of Texas?"

Thoreau's brief reply: "It depends on what they say to each other."

Because speech is so important, it is not surprising that God, in seeking to make himself and his will known in the earth, has chosen to provide His servants with gifts which enable them especially to communicate His gospel through the spoken word.

We shall here consider five such gifts. Some of them overlap with those we discussed in the previous chapter under a different category. It would not only be difficult to separate these gifts one from the other, but they should not be separated.

Most of these offices just considered involved speaking or oral utterance in some manner, but this was not the primary consideration in that category.

Although a gift of communication in writing or by other means might very naturally be connected with the equipping or enabling gifts of the Spirit, we wish now to give special attention to the gifts as they are given for the purpose of *verbalizing truth*. In every instance there will be no other emphasis than on oral communication.

TEACHING

Romans 12:7 and 1 Corinthians 12:28-29

Not only because books were difficult and expensive to produce in the first century, but because teaching is such an effective way of communicating truth, it stands third in Paul's Corinthian list of the gifts. The Holy Spirit has continued to entrust this special gift to individual believers through every age.

In the New Testament era the teacher did not give new or additional revelations of truth as did a prophet. He taught the Scriptures and the doctrines of the faith which had already been given by the Spirit through others. He explained what the prophet had spoken or written. He instructed the believers with clarity and conviction.[1]

Sometimes the teacher uttered the simple, elemental truths of the gospel,[2] and at other times it was much more advanced teaching to the mature believers.[3] In either case, teaching and preaching as gifts of utterance are closely related,[4] and the work of a pastor and teacher are intertwined.

In addition to distinctions that may be made between some of the interrelated gifts, New Testament scholars also distinguish between two types of teaching. They refer to the "proclamation of the gospel to the unregenerate world," and also to the "instruction of the believers in the teachings of the disciples."

Furthermore, it may be observed that teaching proceeds in the church, the Sunday school, the home, and in many other special or unusual settings. Teaching is expounding in detail what may not be possible in preaching, or which may be an integral part of it. It includes powers of understanding, explanation, exposition, and application which must be endowed by the Holy Spirit if spiritual fruit is borne.

It may be noted that a person should employ every means possible to train and discipline the mind and heart for the task of teaching, but then depend upon the Holy Spirit to make it effective by His special gift. The Holy Spirit's work may readily be seen in both the natural and the supernatural realm.[5]

Whereas the purpose of evangelism is to bring new life to those who believe, teaching is primarily for the purpose of sustaining that life. Without teaching there will be little, if any, discipleship.[6] Without teaching spiritual maturity will be slow or not at all.[7]

Teaching must begin immediately after a person comes into a personal relationship with Christ.[8] Paul,[9] Barnabas,[10] Apollos,[11] and others of the New Testament leaders had the gift of teaching. The Holy Spirit saw to it that there were enough teachers to build up the believers in the early church, and He has continued to do so.

Some errors have been made with regard to the gift of teaching. A schoolteacher by profession does not necessarily have the gift of teaching. The gift and the profession of teaching must not be confused. Neither should one conclude that because a person is a good student he will be a good teacher. The two functions are not synonymous nor does one necessarily follow the other. And because a person is available, does not imply that that person is capable or will have the gift of teaching simply on a voluntary basis.

A working definition (as one of the gifts of utterance) is *"Teaching is the ability, plus the supernatural endowment of the Holy Spirit, to acquire and communicate the truth so effectively that believers are led to learn. This in turn promotes growth and the bearing of spiritual fruit."*

EXHORTATION

Romans 12:8

The only specific reference to this gift in the main lists of the gifts is cited in Romans 12:8. The word exhortation stems from the same root as that which is translated "comforter" or "advocate" in reference to the Holy Spirit. The word means to "call for," "summon," or "entreat," and is sometimes translated as encouragement instead of exhortation.

Exhortation is to motivate to action. This gift implies divine enablement for utterance so that people respond positively and practically to the teaching of the word of God. It is this gift which provides the ability to disciple another person in the things of the Lord and to stimulate the faith of others.

147

The purpose and function of exhortation may best be seen in one whose name meant "son of consolation" or "son of one who encourages and exhorts." This was Barnabas[12] whose special gift was exercised when he took Paul under his care[13] and later his young nephew, John Mark.[14]

This gift issues in a ministry which calls forth the best there is in others. It does not imply browbeating or berating another person for his weakness or shortcomings. It does not condemn another person. Rather it lifts up, builds up, encourages, and strengthens other persons to be at their best for the Lord.

Exhortation is a gift which may be exercised either in public or private, but involves utterance, speaking the right words at the right time. This gift helps a person to identify with the needs of another person and to feel with another one very deeply. It is a most practical gift in that it enables a person to respect the dignity and integrity of others. It also combines biblical truths or principles with human experiences in creative, encouraging ways.

Exhortation as a gift, also is the application of challenge or inspiration to a future course of action. The appeal and encouragement may be to service, to ideals of conduct, and to behavior, or to carefulness in Christian living. In a world such as the present, this gift will always be needed in large supply.

Just as the Holy Spirit is the third person of the Holy Trinity, so the Christian believer who is endowed with this gift of the Spirit will have many opportunities of being "called along beside" other people in trouble and need. As a working definition, the gift of exhortation may be regarded as *"the supernatural ability to come alongside to strengthen the weak, to reassure the wavering, to steady the faltering, to console the troubled, to encourage new believers, to comfort the ill, to inspire the halting, and to challenge the backslider."* Not every one who has the gift of exhortation may do all of these things, but some of them will most certainly be done.

PREACHING

Although this term is not specifically used as a distinct gift in any of the New Testament lists, it is so commonly used today that it must be given attention. Preaching is the most general term of all which may include evangelism, pastoring, apostleship, and prophecy. Even exhorting and teaching may involve preaching, but it would more likely be in reverse order, that is to say, when one is given the gift of preaching, both teaching and exhorting may also be a part of the preaching function.

Preaching is properly considered as the

ability to utter with both clarity and poignancy the truth of God's Word for the purpose of evangelism, of comforting the afflicted and afflicting the comfortable, of challenging to greater service, of inspiring to more holy living, and of stimulating believers to go on to perfection, holiness, and maturity.

Basic to the effective utterance of God's truth as a preacher-prophet-evangelist-pastor is the disposition and attitude of *study* and learning to "show thyself approved unto God, a workman that needeth not to be ashamed, rightly dividing the word of truth" (2 Timothy 2:15). With adequate preparation, prayerful study of God's Word, and the humble dependence upon God's Holy Spirit to give expression, the minister may experience the particular, peculiar anointing of the Spirit which establishes rapport with the hearers, which enables the delivery of the truth with pungency, resulting in Spirit-directed action. This may very well be the gift of the Spirit at a time for a given number of needs, often called "the anointing of the Spirit." If not synonymous with or identical to the gift of the Spirit for preaching, it is at least most commensurate with the whole task of preaching.

LANGUAGES

Acts 2:5-12; 10:44-46; 19:6;
1 Corinthians 12:10, 28; 14:1-40

We will spend a little extra space dealing

with this gift and the next one, interpretation. The current church scene requires us to give special consideration, because of the great disagreement, division, and even strife which surround the understanding and use of these two gifts. It is certainly unfortunate that two gifts of the Holy Spirit, given for the extension and the upbuilding of the kingdom have come into such harsh situations.

The first thing which should be said is that it is difficult for most North Americans to understand the need and use of these particular gifts. North Americans live in a culture dominated by one or two languages. They can preach, teach, and witness generally unhampered by the hearers' inability to understand what is being said. Modern communication has brought a semblance of unity of language. This is not so in some parts of the world today, and it was especially untrue of the world 2,000 years ago.

The New Testament world was one where myriads of languages and dialects existed. Many of the major cities of the time literally teamed with people speaking scores of different languages and dialects.

Into this world of a multitude of dialects and languages came the gospel of Jesus Christ. Christianity was not to be a national or clannish religion — but a universal one, open to all people of all nations and languages. The problem: how does this universal gospel get communicated to the various peoples of the world, all speaking different languages?

A further problem was that the initial followers of Jesus of Nazareth were not cosmopolitan men of multilingual capacities. These simple men were given the task of preaching the gospel of Jesus Christ to the entire world. And if the church was to make it through the first few centuries of mass martyrdoms it must have a good start — conversions by the thousands not dozens.

Thus, given the multilingual makeup of the world, and the huge preaching mission of the followers of Jesus, and of the urgency of the task, it does not surprise us that the gifts of unlearned languages and interpretation were two very necessary and used gifts during these times.

The multilingual situation has changed in many parts of the world during the 2,000 intervening years, but the gifts of languages and interpretation are still needed in many places where communicating the gospel in a language readily understandable by the hearers is vital. During the reading of the remainder of this chapter it will help the reader to keep in mind these situations where this gift is in special demand.

The current widespread consideration of this gift has brought into rather common use the New Testament Greek term *glossolalia* to describe "speaking in tongues" — speaking in unlearned foreign languages. Tongues-speaking was not a universal phenomenon in the New Testament church, but there seems little doubt that this gift in the book of Acts refers to the ability given the apostles to speak in unlearned languages or dialects. The purpose in each case was to clearly and precisely communicate the truth of God to people of diverse languages. Those present in Jerusalem on the Day of Pentecost were from a dozen or fifteen different nations with varying languages. At the house of Cornelius in Caesarea and at Ephesus there were also language barriers which would have prevented hearers from understanding what was transpiring. Therefore, the apostles were supernaturally endowed with the ability to speak and/or for the hearers to hear in the dialects with which they were familiar and which the apostles had never studied or learned — thus the gift title of "unlearned languages."

The record in Acts makes it clear that there were no "unknown" tongues involved. They were known by the hearers. The fact is the gift was given to *prevent* unknown tongues. The purpose was to help everyone understand. To identify them as unknown languages "is to fly in the face of both reason and scripture and can result in only confusion."[15]

The major purpose of *glossolalia,* or the use of unlearned languages in the book of Acts was evidential and authenticating. Some authorities conclude that this was the only reason for the gift and that it disappeared with the apostolic leaders and that this gift ended once and for all time. Such a position, however, is not necessary to guard against the abuse or misuse of this or any other gift of the Spirit. It also is a denial of the right of the Holy Spirit to endow His servants with whatever gift He pleases.

It must be noted that the record shows that missionaries and other ministers of the gospel, as well as lay persons, have been given on special occasions the supernatural ability to communicate effectively in an unlearned language.

Some common errors with reference to the gift of speaking in unlearned languages must be avoided. *One common error is that this gift is an evidence of the baptism with the Holy Spirit.* Everyone who is a believer certainly has the privilege of being baptized with the Holy Spirit. It is the Christian's right by the new birth also to be filled with the Holy Spirit or baptized in the Spirit or by the Spirit. But no one single gift, besides the Holy Spirit himself, has been promised to all believers.

It should be noted also that the Old Testament prophets foretold all of the essential characteristics of the age of the Holy Spirit. They told of the fruitfulness and blessing which would prevail, of the cleansing, the freedom in prayer, the law of God written in the soul, with the accompanying grace and vision, but they make no mention of any sign such as *glossolalia*.

Furthermore, Jesus who had a full measure of the Spirit[16] is nowhere said to have spoken in any other language than his native Aramaic tongue. And in all of His teachings concerning the coming of the Spirit in His Last Supper conversations (John 14—16) He does not mention any confirming linguistic sign. Surely any doctrine to be considered essential must find its roots in Jesus' own teachings.

In the book of Acts there are numerous references to the fullness of the Spirit in addition to the occasions mentioned[17] and in none of them is there any allusion to tongues-speaking. So it is an error to teach that any gift is proof of the baptism with the Holy Spirit.

Another common error is to conclude that the gift of speaking in unlearned languages or the use of an unknown tongue as a special prayer language is a means of spiritual growth and maturity. For the Holy Spirit to endow a person with a gift of any kind as an evidence of His presence or as a means of attaining spiritual maturity is unbiblical. Also, since speaking in unlearned languages is quite spectacular in itself, there is grave danger that personal pride or division among the members of the body of Christ can occur, or that the genuine gift exercised in the early church as recorded in Acts may become a spurious or counterfeit variety. Such occurrences of the spurious plagued the New

Testament church in Corinth and continues to plague the church even to the present.

Many non-Christian and even nonreligious people have spoken in some kind of spurious vocalizations just as many have performed miracles. Since this is the case, it is clearly possible for a carnal, immature, or unsuspecting Christian to be led into a supposed gift. The least that can be said is that this is not what Luke recorded as happening at Pentecost, at the house of Cornelius, or at Ephesus.

Every gift must be exercised in love and in the unity of the Spirit or one can safely conclude it is not of the Spirit. He is not the author of confusion or disunity. Where the Spirit of the Lord is, there is liberty with unity, not undisciplined freedom with division in the body.

Some 20 years after Pentecost the Apostle Paul found it necessary to write to the believers at Corinth relative to tongues-speaking, because *glossolalia* had become a critical issue in the ailing, divided church. Paul wrote about the phenomenon not because it was such a blessing, but because it had become such a grave problem.

Corinth, an important commercial seaport of which peoples from all parts of the world made their way, was perhaps even more than Jerusalem, Caesarea, and Ephesus, characterized by a varied, rapidly changing populace. "Consequently *there is good reason to assume that a bona fide gift of different languages may have occurred in the church of Corinth to meet the need for evangelization of this transient population."*[18]

As in Acts, so in Paul's Corinthian letter, the word "unknown" does not appear in connection with "tongue" in the Greek text. Unfortunately, it does appear in the King James Version of 1 Corinthians 14. But even there it is italicized to indicate that it does not appear in the original Greek of the New Testament but was added by the translators in an attempt to clarify the meaning of the word. This was unfortunate for it does not appear in the standard modern translations. Apparently, there were those persons in the Corinthian church who were counterfeiting the genuine gifts. It seems that others who had been converted out of pagan religions where unintelligible, ecstatic utterance, and trances were a common part of worship, had in the confusion introduced elements of those pagan practices into Christian worship.

Doubtless then the use of speech or verbal sounds employed at Corinth generally produced no positive benefit among the believers. It was for this reason, because there was the misuse, abuse, and prostitution of a genuine gift, which gave no benefit to the believers or unbelievers, that Paul approached the subject.

The true test in Paul's directive to the Corinthians was that *to qualify as a gift it must be directed outwardly.* If others are not edified by the use of the unlearned language, then it is not a true gift. This is the case with all other gifts of the Spirit as well. They cannot be regarded as gifts of the Spirit if this is not true. This was the case in the Corinthian church. A self-advertising, self-exalting phenomenon was in vogue at Corinth, which Paul condemned. He did not rule out a true gift of speaking in unlearned languages, but relegated it to the end of the list as being rarely needed or used, even in his era. This is borne out in the fact that Paul did not need the gift nor was it given to him by the Holy Spirit, or to any of the other apostles after the cases named in Acts.

We must insist, as does the Apostle Paul in 1 Corinthians 14, that communication among the believers or to the unregenerate world must be with clarity and with understanding. The clear presentation of the truth in the vernacular of the hearer is to be insisted upon, as over against incomprehensible, ecstatic speech. It may well be repeated over and over that the purpose of the Holy Spirit is to exalt the Lord Christ, to bring the words that He spoke to the understanding of the hearer, and in the bestowal of the gifts to edify, build up, and fortify the Christian family for its great task of spreading the gospel.

The exhortation of the Apostle Paul may well be the best conclusion to the matter, "I . . . entreat you to walk in a manner worthy of

the calling with which you have been called . . .
being diligent to preserve the unity of the Spirit
in the bond of peace" (Ephesians 4:1, 3, NASB).
Thus, true spirituality has no inherent relationship to any one or all of the gifts of the Spirit.
The Holy Spirit produces His fruit in the life of
the believer as He is given time and opportunity to do so. When he has His way in heart and
life, He brings the believer into conformity with
the image of Christ.

INTERPRETATION OF LANGUAGES
1 Corinthians 12:10

The last of the gifts in Paul's list in the Corinthians correspondence should be related to
and connected with the former gift of speaking
in unlearned languages.

The reason for this seems to be clear and
that is because, if the gift of speaking in unlearned languages is just that, it implies that the
one speaking does not even know or understand the language which he is using. This
necessitates the use of another gift of the Spirit
which Paul insists upon so that the hearers may
understand the message which the Spirit wishes
to communicate. *Interpretation is the gift of
translating a spoken message into a language
readily understood by the hearer.*

This may partially be understood by the
present-day use of an interpreter by evangelists

and missionaries. Although the speaker is speaking intelligently in his own language, the hearers would not be able to understand the speaker if it were not for an interpreter. That the Holy Spirit endows such interpreters with the gift, not only to give the sense of the message as accurately as possible, but also to catch the spirit and truth of the message so that even that communication is possible by the Spirit, from speaker through interpreter to hearer.

"Spiritual insight and inspiration often play a far more important role in efficient interpretation than simply a thorough knowledge of two languages" — Charles W. Carter.

I believe a safe conclusion to the matter of languages and the gifts associated with them is that there is a genuine gift as demonstrated in Acts and that such speaking in unlearned languages is of God, and that other speaking in so-called languages is not of God and therefore invalid in the church or among believers anywhere.

The most obvious reason for the gift of interpretation is so that people may comprehend what is being said; but more than this, it turns the focus from the speaker and the unlearned language which is being spoken to the message which the Holy Spirit is trying to communicate in the speaker. Principles for the use of unlearned languages are very carefully laid down by Paul in 1 Corinthians 14. The least that can be said is that the gifts are not to be sought, whether it is one of the first or one of the last on the list. The Holy Spirit has full control of the gifts, and He does not direct us to seek them. And the gifts of the Spirit are not to be relied upon as an evidence of salvation, maturity, or spirituality.

SUMMARY

The human faculty of speech distinguishes man from all other creatures of the earth, and is a basic element in the meaningful communication which makes civilization possible. God has recognized the importance of this and has granted gifts by which to facilitate oral communication in the work of His kingdom.

He has provided the gift of speaking effectively in teaching the truth He has revealed in His Word. God has granted the gift of exhortation which enables the speaker to communicate understandingly and sensitively to those who need spiritual help. He is able thereby to awaken, comfort, encourage, and inspire.

There is a gift of preaching which may well include those of teaching and exhorting. By this God's chosen persons are able to reach out to the unconverted and to stimulate and challenge believers on unto holiness and maturity. Then, to make possible cross-cultural communication God has provided some of His workers with the gift of speaking in languages which they have not learned. And to others He has granted the gift to interpret spoken languages to persons who would not otherwise understand.

All of these utterance gifts are to bring about greater understanding and unity among the members of Christ's church and are able to be used in taking the gospel meaningfully to persons who have not heard.

What Do You Think About These?

1. Why are the gifts of utterance so important in the work of building God's kingdom upon the earth?

2. What are the basic gifts of utterance?

3. What is the function of each of these gifts?

If You Want to Dig a Little Deeper

1. In the light of your study on this chapter, list the gifts of utterance, define each in your own words, and cite at least one scripture passage to illustrate each.

Bible References Relating to This Chapter

[1] 2 Timothy 2:2
[2] Hebrews 5:12
[3] Hebrews 5:14
[4] 2 Timothy 4:2
[5] Matthew 13:52; John 14:26
[6] Matthew 28:19-20
[7] Colossians 1:28
[8] Acts 2:41-42
[9] 2 Timothy 1:11
[10] Acts 15:35
[11] Acts 18:24-25
[12] Acts 4:36
[13] Acts 9:27
[14] Acts 15:39
[16] John 3:34
[17] Acts 1:5,8; 4:8, 31; 5:32; 6:3, 5; 8:15, 17-19; 9:17; 11:15-16, 24; 13:9, 52; 15:8

Bibliography

[15] Purkiser, W. T. — The Gifts of the Spirit, page 56.
[18] Carter, Charles W. — The Person and Ministry of the Holy Spirit, page 206.

THE SERVING GIFTS

Relevant Scriptures: Romans 12:3-8; 1 Corinthians 12:8-10, 28-30; 1 Peter 4:10-11.

Becoming a Christian involves conversion, but it just as surely involves a commission.

The Apostle Paul suggests that when in writing to the Ephesian Christians he declared that a primary work of church leaders is "to prepare God's people for works of service" (Ephesians 4:12, NIV).

So it is that every believer has a commission to serve somewhere, somehow.

Indeed, the vitality and strength of the church depends upon every member seeing himself as a person called of God and gladly engaging himself daily in some kingdom service.

The standard of achievement in the kingdom is ministering to or serving others. Christ taught this not only by precept,[1] but also by His example generally, and He illustrated it specifically when He took a towel and washed His disciples' feet.[2]

In accordance with this principle, the Holy Spirit endows every believer with at least one gift. Some of these gifts are so particularly related to service that they can be examined together. We shall now consider those serving gifts.

WISDOM

1 Corinthians 12:8

By the gift of the "word of wisdom" Paul apparently means the doctrine of wisdom, for he used the Greek word *logos* which appears in numerous places in the New Testament to imply "doctrine" or "teaching." In this sense it refers to what Adam Clarke calls the wisdom of "the mystery of our redemption, in which the wisdom of God was most eminently conspicuous."

Jesus promised the word of wisdom to believers when He forewarned His disciples of impending cross-examination of their faith by the world.[3] On several occasions in Acts believers spoke with wisdom beyond themselves. Peter had the right words to lay on the religious leaders in Acts 4:8-12, so that they marveled.

The Greek word, *sophia*, also is used in this context. It is defined or translated as "insight," "understanding," "judgment," or "the ability to grasp the real heart and essence of things." The

Bible has much to say about wisdom and man's need for it.

It begins with the "fear of the Lord" (Proverbs 9:10) and continues in the hearts of the humble as a divinely imparted gift. It may appropriately be observed that the modern scientific movement, with the increase of knowledge about the world and ourselves, has tended to rule out the exercise of such wisdom. As stated by P. T. Forsythe, "Men are too clever ever to be wise."

The gift of wisdom has to do with spiritual illumination which enables a believer to apply God's truth to a given need or problem. The use of this gift will be recognized by others because they see the application of spiritual truth in a special manner to a concrete experience.

Although all Christians are urged to ask for wisdom when they need it (James 1:5), this is not to be understood as a biblical basis for seeking any one or all of the gifts of the Spirit. The gift of wisdom as listed by Paul in 1 Corinthians 12:8, is a special power given only to some Christians for a given service to be given in a spiritually relevant situation.

Paul's strongest words about wisdom are found in 1 Corinthians 1:17—2:16. He indicates that even the untrained in theology or those of little if any formal academic training may and do possess this gift. It is not to be concluded that study and training are unnecessary, but that the

Holy Spirit gives this gift to many lay people, as well as ministers, and to the less wise, as far as the world's wisdom is concerned, as well as to some with advanced formal training.

Jesus exercised this gift repeatedly when Jewish leaders tried to trap Him in an obtuse question or situation. His answers were with such apparent insight that His opponents were rebuked, if not satisfied and silenced. All believers are exhorted to be prepared always to give an answer to everyone who asks them to give a reason for the hope they have (1 Peter 3:15, NIV). Everyone may call on the Lord in such an hour for such an answer, but special ability and a gift of wisdom is given to some to meet and refute the attacks or arguments of unbelievers and gainsayers.

KNOWLEDGE

1 Corinthians 12:8

The word of wisdom and the word of knowledge should be understood both in contrast and in comparison. Whereas the word of wisdom seems to involve the application of a spiritual truth, the word of knowledge implies the ability to perceive a fact as God reveals it.

The two gifts may at times be committed to the same person. When this is true, the gifts complement each other. Because a person has the understanding of a fact does not necessarily imply that he has the ability to use or apply the insight in a practical way to meet a need or solve a problem (wisdom).

Examples of Jesus' use of this gift are numerous.[4] We see the gift in use also in the life of Peter.[5] This gift is not understood to be a divine amplification of human knowledge, nor is it knowledge which can be gained by study. *Knowledge must be understood as a supernatural revelation of some fact known by God alone which He intends for the profit and edification of His body, the Church.*

To grasp and communicate knowledge relates to the human qualities of intelligence and mental prowess. But the gift of knowledge is more than innate intelligence. It is the Spirit's energizing power communicated through a human channel of understanding open to His use.

Just as knowledge implies personal involvement, so the gift of the Spirit is not given for the sake of information alone. It is given with the incentive for action. In this case, for service to the body of Christ. Thus the gift of knowledge is instrumental and means that God intends the word, the doctrine, or the teaching imparted, to be used in pleasing Him through service to mankind.

FAITH

1 Corinthians 12:9

This is not saving faith in general, which is

the common endowment of all Christians, but rather wonder-working faith. This gift is of the mountain-moving variety.[6] _Faith is a Spirit-given ability to believe that something God wants done can be done and that He will sustain that unwavering confidence which accomplishes the task in spite of seeming insurmountable obstacles._

Hardly one commentator or serious theologian defines the gift of faith without giving the illustration of it in the life of Stephen[7] and in the ministry of George Muller, who cared for 10,000 orphans over a period of 60 years from faith income of some five million dollars. The gift of faith prompts prayers of gratitude for the fact before it is visible to human sense, like that of Jesus when He raised Lazarus from the dead.[8]

Faith in general is experienced in varying degrees by all Christians. Without faith it is impossible to please God at all. The people of faith in Hebrews 11, were persons who lived victoriously by faith. In specific instances they may have had the special spiritual gift of faith mentioned by Paul. This spiritual gift, like all others, comes only by the sovereign bestowal of the Spirit. It cannot be exercised as a person may please. It is usually related to some total human impossibility or crisis when the Spirit wills to perform something for the edification and benefit of the believers.

The spiritual gift of faith is not the same as

that which grows in a normal relationship with Christ, as it is listed as a fruit of the Spirit in Galatians 5:22 by Paul and in 2 Peter 1:5 where Peter is urging growth and development. In such instances the better usage is "faithfulness" rather than faith, even in the normal sense of the word.

The spiritual gift of faith, then, is given to some Christians, not all, as a special ability to see the adequacy of God for a given situation and to draw upon the divine resources to see His will accomplished in normally impossible ways. It is involved in extraordinary answers to prayer. It is generated by the Word of God, but it is a direct gift of the Spirit.

HEALING

1 Corinthians 12:9, 28

Although great admiration and appreciation is due those wonderful people who are involved professionally in the healing arts and who have developed great skills in medical science, this gift of the Spirit involves much more. The Greek word here is plural in its form, so that it is properly "gifts of healing."

In accord with the formula stated by James 9, it appears that faith for a specific healing will be given by the Spirit as believers pray for the need of a person. And there is no evidence that healing refers only to physical ills. *Healing is the supernatural mending of the spirit, mind, or body.*

It must also be noted that God uses different means to bring about healing.

Because there are frauds and counterfeits among the so-called "healers" should not deter Christian believers in allowing the Spirit of God to work out His will. Gifts of healings are an authentic part of God's plan to meet the needs of persons and thereby to edify the church. But it is also a presumption upon God to insist on telling Him when and how to heal the body, mind, or soul. Persons to whom God imparts the special gifts of healings will place faith in God and trust Him for the results.

MIRACLES

1 Corinthians 12:10,28

This expression is the same as that in verse 6 of this same chapter, where "workings" or "operations" of the Spirit is the proper translation. Our English word for energy comes from the same root in the Greek, and it is used only by Paul with reference to superhuman strength, energy, or power.

The miracles, workings, or operations of the Spirit are not so much a specific gift, as they seem to refer to the result of His power flowing through believers' lives in the gifts of faith and healings. But there is no question that there are miracles of all types and descriptions among believers today. There are definitely supernatural interventions in many areas of life to the believer and spiritually aware. Miracles are not simply natural occurrences seen through consecrated eyes, as some humanists would argue. The very essence of a miracle is that it cannot be explained on the basis of natural, ordinary phenomena. When it can be explained by natural, scientific means, a miracle ceases to be a miracle.

The gift of miracles, or gifts which result in the miraculous, is closely related to the former gifts of healings, for both are supernatural interventions in the ordinary course of things. But since Paul makes two statements to describe the work of the Spirit, a differentiation between healings and miracles may be made. *Gifts of healing primarily relate to those divine acts which result in the cure of mental, emotional, or physical and spiritual maladies. In contrast, the gift of miracles includes these acts plus all other divine acts which may transcend or interrupt the stream of natural experiences.*

It is well to note that all over the world among Christian believers, the mighty workings of the Spirit are occurring for which there are no solely human causes. These are not only physical, but as has been noted, they are also psychological and spiritual.

DISCERNMENT

1 Corinthians 12:10

This is the gift by which the Spirit enables a

171

believer to discern a false miracle from a genuine one or to recognize a false prophet from one who is truly of God. It may also include such ability as was given to Peter in the case of Ananias and Sapphira.[10]

The Greek is translated as discerning or distinguishing of or between spirits. The term implies decision, separation, discrimination, and determination with regard to things of a spiritual nature. This is best understood in the light of Christ's warnings about many false prophets, doing great things to fascinate and charm the unsuspecting, and also John's admonition in his first epistle, "Dear friends, do not believe every spirit, but test the spirits to see whether they are from God, because many false prophets have gone out into the world" (1 John 4:1, NIV).

In the cosmic conflict between God and Satan, the latter does not always oppose God directly, but tries, as Paul warns, to impede by counterfeiting the true.[11] In view of the powers and principalities in the spiritual world, *God has given to some persons the ability to discriminate between the spirit of truth and the spirit of error, between what is truly of God and what is only pretense or sham.*[12]

It is obvious that the purpose of this gift is to keep Satan's influence from causing serious and permanent problems in the body of Christ. The gift is not related to natural abilities, training, or insight, although the Holy Spirit may find willingness to employ whatever is committed to Him. The ability is given by the Spirit at a time it is needed. Without the gift of discernment the people of God would be open to all sorts of odd teachings, false doctrines, and those who pose as genuine spiritual leaders who are not.[13]

HELPS

Romans 12:7; 1 Corinthians 23:28;
1 Peter 4:11

The gift of helps is described by two different Greek terms. In the Romans and 1 Peter contexts the word has the same root as the word for deacon, meaning service or ministry. In 1 Corinthians the word implies a service rendered to the poor and sick by the deacons. The same word occurs in Luke 1:54 and in Romans 8:26, where God's Servant and His Spirit are said to help Israel and to help us in our infirmities when we pray.

Some authorities believe the gift of helps may refer to the apostles' helpers who accompanied them and did the many things the former could not do or get done while their time was taken in other spiritual duties. In any event the meaning of both usages noted above involves the idea of helpers who carry the burden of another person. God gives to many people the ability to sense the needs of others and to do something concrete about those needs.

173

There may be a difference between the specific gift of helps and the gift of serving, but they are closely related and overlap in their effects among believers. Helps may be more person-centered while service may be more task-oriented. The effects of these activities can blend well in the edification of believers.

Neither of these gifts may have the glamour of publicity, but both are indispensable to the life of the church.[14] Persons who have the gift of helps are equipped to relieve temporal and spiritual needs. This gift enables a person to respond without urging to the opportunity of helping. It is a voluntary service, willingly given without thought of reward. At least part of this concept was involved in the work of the early church when the seven deacons were set apart for services and ministries which the apostles did not have time to accomplish.[15]

While engaged in a weekend Bible conference, the writer witnessed a teenage girl, although rather reserved and with few apparent endowments, demonstrate the gift of helps. About halfway through the service, the pastor's small son became ill and lost his supper in the pew and down the side aisle before his mother could get him to the rest room. While every other person in the church sat frozen in their seats, the young girl quickly and with an armful of the right things to use for such an emergency, proceeded quietly to clean every remnant of the accident. Just as quietly she returned to her seat and listened to the rest of the message as though nothing had happened. When the service was over and this writer was loading the car with numerous materials, this same young lady was there, without invitation or comment simply going about doing what needed to be done.

She had a gift which was precious, and when the writer took time to comment on it with praise to the Lord, she responded humbly with a shy smile and the words, "That makes me so happy to know it is a gift of God to help other people."

The gift of helps, then, is the Spirit-given ability to give a supporting role, usually temporal, but sometimes spiritual, to others. The gift enables one to give support and service joyfully and diligently in such activities as providing flowers, providing transportation for shut-ins, distributing brochures, preparing food or cleaning up after a meal for the church, improving the church grounds or lending a hand to a neighbor in need, working in the church nursery, ushering, decorating, driving the church bus, shoveling snow in the winter, or cutting the grass in summer — anything that will bring encouragement, beauty, or strength to others.

ADMINISTRATION

Romans 12:8; 1 Corinthians 12:28

Again there are two concepts involved in the two passages from which leadership, ruling, and government as a gift of the Spirit is drawn. No ecclesiastical office is intended, but rather a general reference to any responsibility involving superintendence, as the meaning of Paul's statement in Romans.

In the Corinthian passage it is a reference "probably to administrators of church government, as presbyters," inasmuch as the root term is drawn from the shipping business. In that setting it means a shipmaster or steersman. It is a person who has the ability of leadership. It may be the earliest example of a simile which was used rather widely by Christian writers later in comparing the church to a ship which needed steersmen.

The biblical principle of orderliness commits the church to organization and a certain amount of administration.[16] Administration is more than organization. _Administration is the God-given ability to guide, to govern, to rule, to pilot, to preside, or to direct and lead a segment of the whole body of Christ._ It does not imply manipulation or the human tendency to "rule over." The disciples of Christ had to be taught that leadership could not be equated with position, power, glory, or greatness. They were not to lord it over those who were given them to lead.[17]

An important principle of the Christian faith is ignored when men strive for leadership in the church. Those who seek for position will probably not be given the gift, however much natural ability they have. Leadership must be seen as an opportunity to serve. It must not be identified with greatness, with position or personality, or with the ability to speak eloquently to persuade them.

Leaders or would-be leaders should give diligent attention to Paul's directives to leaders in the church.[18] Those who are given the gift of administration will also be given ability to exercise leadership in love, if they will permit the Spirit to teach them. A rigid dogmatism, an unkind dominance, or a determined authoritarianism will cool the ardor of the most loyal and spiritually minded believer. It is the duty of administrators to serve with humility, love, and wisdom, while seeking to coordinate the gifts and ministries of others for the common good. The result of the operation of this gift will be smooth and efficient operation of the church for the glory of Christ and the good of the believers.

Church administration, when Spirit-directed and endowed, is never dogmatic, demagogic, or dictatorial. It expresses itself rather in wisdom, tact, humility, and loving service.

GIVING
Romans 12:8

Paul states that one who has the gift of giving should exercise it with simplicity. This means with singleness of mind and heart, without pretense or parade. When a person donates or gives with generosity, liberality, and delight, the conditions set forth by Christ and Paul will undoubtedly be met.[19]

Although giving is a gift of the Spirit, it does not mean that only the wealthy have it. Some of the poorest of God's own are given this gift; and no one is excused from giving as the Lord has prospered him.[20] Giving material or financial aid is a responsibility of every Christian, because each one is a steward of the things God has given him, whether many or few.

Those who are sensitive to the needs of others and who are prompted by the Spirit with the joyful opportunity to give aid exercise this gift. The late R. G. LeTourneau and Mr. Stanley Tam are examples of men who in sincerity and humility have had great resources entrusted to them and who in turn have used them for the glory of God. There are many who have given out of their wealth from a philanthropic heart. That is good, but the gift of giving implies more than a love of fellowmen. It means giving with a heart full of the love of God with no regard to recognition and without selfish calculation of any kind.

It should also be noted that the gift of giving involves or may lead to real sacrifice. It is not generous to give what one will never miss or what is not needed. The test of this gift must come at the point of the advancement of God's kingdom with such wisdom and cheerfulness that believers are blessed and strengthened.

SHOWING MERCY
Romans 12:8

Acts of mercy are those done by a gracious heart of understanding, concern, and empathy toward the miserable. Although every Christian is to be merciful,[21] this is a special gift of the Spirit as a divine enablement to be a channel of God's mercy in times of special need.

To the wretched, the unworthy, handicapped, and miserable the Holy Spirit will enable a person by His gift of mercy to show compassion through deeds of kindness with hilarity! As one authority says, the Greek *hilaritas* denotes "the joyful eagerness, the amiable grace, the affability going the length of gaiety, which make the visitor a sunbeam penetrating into the sick-chamber, and to the heart of the afflicted."

Another says, that "hilarity goes well with true and undefiled religion. Frivolity in the

Christian church is a denial of religion; hilarity is its sure evidence. Humor in its true use of it springs out of the peace of God."

The verb which is translated "show mercy" may also be accurately translated "to pity," "to commiserate," "to have compassion on," "to show gracious favor to." This gift involves more than the stirring of the emotions. _It is the gift of a deep-down compassion of supernatural origin._ It is the Spirit of Jesus who was moved with compassion when He saw the multitudes scattered as sheep without a shepherd.[22]

It is compassion defined as "your pain in my heart!" It is God's love, under the Spirit's guidance, acting in Christ's name, for the glory of God, relieving the pain, misery, loneliness, grief, suffering, heartache, hurt, and ill of one's fellowmen. If they are not relieved, at least mercy has been demonstrated in acts and deeds that are ungrudgingly and joyfully rendered.

Doing mercy with a grudge and a growl cancels out the service intended. But doing deeds of mercy may be one of the most effective and the strongest of Christian witnesses to an unregenerate, unbelieving world. Opportunities for the exercise of this gift are unlimited in a world that is hurting and bleeding, in an age that is dry-eyed and hard-nosed so far as the spiritual needs are concerned.

Although secular social work and welfare programs for the needy are commendable and worthy pursuits, it is the Christian believers in the body of Christ who should be the primary agency for serving and ministering to the physical and temporal needs of others. Helping others in distress is a more-important role than preaching or teaching them the truth at that point.

SUMMARY

Though all Christians are to serve other persons as representatives of their Lord, some specialized service gifts have been granted by the Holy Spirit to provide for His church's needs.

The spiritual gift of wisdom provides insight into the mysteries of salvation along with the capacity to grasp the real heart of a situation and apply God's truth to it. So, among other things, it qualifies the believer wisely to answer those who would oppose the truth of God.

There is the gift of knowledge which furnishes the recipient with the ability to perceive facts and to act upon those facts in service to others.

While there are the gifts which enable some to achieve unusual things through faith, and to bring about healings and miracles, there are also those whom God has just as truly gifted to serve inobtrusively in obscure places. These latter may be less heralded, but their work is no less essential if the church is to function smoothly and have the outreach it should.

Some are enabled by a special gift to administer organizational affairs wisely while others are enabled to give to their support. Still others are made particularly sensitive to the human needs of others and are able to show compassion and mercy to the glory of the Lord.

As the members of the body of Christ exercise these gifts faithfully the church is able in each generation to minister to the needs of the world.

What Do You Think of These?

1. Have you seen any of these serving gifts being exercised in the church? Which ones?

2. If so, what have been the results of that exercise?

If You Want to Dig a Little Deeper

You have studied three categories of spiritual gifts: equipping gifts, gifts of utterance, and serving gifts. Make lists of those gifts under each category. Note those gifts which appear in more than one category and explain in your own words how they either supplement or complement each other.

Bible References Relating to This Chapter
[1]Matthew 20:26
[2]John 13:12-16
[3]Matthew 10:19-20

4Matthew 21:2; John 4:16-26
5Matthew 16:16-17; Acts 5:1-3
61 Corinthians 13:2
7Acts 6:8ff.
8John 11:41-42
9James 5:14-15
10Acts 5:1ff.
112 Corinthians 11:14-15
12Ephesians 6:12
131 Timothy 4:1
141 Corinthians 12:19-22
15Acts 6:2-5
161 Corinthians 14:40
17Mark 10:42-44
181 Timothy 3:1-13
19Matthew 6:3; 2 Corinthians 9:7
201 Corinthians 16:1ff.
21Luke 6:36
22Matthew 9:36

DISCOVERING AND DEVELOPING SPIRITUAL GIFTS

Relevant Scriptures: Acts 8:4-8, 26-40; Romans 1:11-12; 12:3-8; Colossians 4:17; 1 Timothy 4:12-16; 6:20-21; 2 Timothy 1:6-14; 4:1-5; James 5:15.

It is one thing to be aware of what the spiritual gifts are as listed in various passages of Scripture. It is quite another to know how they are being used presently in one's own life.

Admittedly, the real issue is not, "What is my gift?" or "What are your gifts?" The Lord knows how to reveal His will and His way to the committed; and He will do so in His good pleasure. The primary issue is to make oneself available for whatever it is the Lord wills. This should be understood clearly, before pressing on to study the matter of discovery of spiritual gifts.

First of all, the Holy Spirit does not ignore your personal delights as a fully committed Christian. What you enjoy doing may be a clue to what it is the Spirit may be doing through you without your knowledge of its full impact on others.

Next, one must recognize that no one has all of the gifts. Everyone needs other persons, and all must be bound together by love. Caution must be urged against becoming so engrossed in discovering gifts that no actual use is made of them.

But over against this caution, it is a matter of record that Paul urged Timothy more than once to highly regard the things that had been committed to him.[1] Archippus also was exhorted to give diligent attention to what was given him.[2]

Another significant principle to follow in discovering one's gift or gifts is to get into the arena of service. It is often as we go to work for the Lord that the Spirit shows what He wants us to do. This is not to be a hit-and-miss kind of service. It is to do regularly what is at hand. It involves taking advantage of every opportunity. Part of any gift is a spiritual sensitivity. If that sensitivity is not present, one will not even be aware of the need.

Willingness to try something new may sometimes uncover a work of the Spirit that would never have been known. Exposure to various kinds of service will also give one opportunities for the Spirit to supply a gift. When Paul exhorted Timothy to do all the things named in 2 Timothy 4:1-5, was he hinting that Timothy might discover a ministry for which the Spirit would supply a gift? It is possible that many gifts the Spirit would like to give cannot be endowed because of a person's reservations about his own natural abilities.

When God desires a certain ministry to be performed He most assuredly will equip His people with the corresponding gift. In turn, He will open doors of opportunity to minister in that way. He will also incline His chosen one to perform that task. To a certain degree, then, the person who has a desire and willingness to serve in a specific way may well have the gift of the Spirit to accompany that openness to do His will. There are a few expressions in Paul's letters that indicate we should desire the best gifts.[3]

The above statements do not preclude the overriding factor that the Holy Spirit makes the final assignment of gifts and that they are not awarded on the basis of individual desire.[4]

In addition to the awareness of what the gifts of the Spirit are — a willingness and desire to do what God wishes, taking advantage of opportunities to serve whatever they may be — there must be prayer and faith with common sense or understanding of what God is doing through the yielding heart. To manifest His workings and to show His will, God more often uses the things at hand than by a flash from heaven or a mysterious voice of some kind.

The needs of others as well as one's own de-

sires and pleasures in God's service are keys to God's endowments. Past ministries and experiences may also well add to the evidence that God has given you a certain gift or various gifts.

The observations and evaluations of spiritually discerning people are also helpful in determining one's gift or gifts, as long as the human understanding is taken for what it is — just that and only that. How is it that other people think about a certain person? For what do people ask of that person? What do others say? What kinds of assignments are made to that person? Answers to these questions may indicate a certain gift.

Another important matter to keep in mind is that *spiritual gifts, like physical maturation, do not come to the point of discovery all at once.* It usually takes time for a maturing Christian to discover and identify the spiritual gifts he may possess. Questions one may ask about gifts include:

1. In what areas is a personal competence developing?

2. In what ways can I now exercise this gift?

3. Where are results appearing in the lives of others with whom I serve and try to work?

4. Have other people in whom I have utmost confidence given me special encouragement in certain areas where I have served?

5. What is the witness of the Holy Spirit to my life in a personal way?

6. In areas where I have served is there a unity and harmony within the body of believers?

RECOGNIZING SPIRITUAL GIFTS

Acts 8:4-8; 8:26-40; Romans 12:3-8

The example of Philip and his ministry after Pentecost indicates that others recognized his spiritual gifts, both at Samaria and in individual exposition to the Ethiopian eunuch. The expression of "spiritual gifts" is not used in the passages from Acts, but the implication is the same as that of Paul to the Romans when he exhorts them to recognize and use the gifts they have (Romans 12:6).

Dr. K. C. Kinghorn gives the following summary of the ways spiritual gifts may be discovered and recognized:

● Open yourself to God as a channel for His use.

● Examine your aspirations for Christian service and ministry.

● Identify the needs most crucial in the life of the church.

● Evaluate the results of your efforts to serve and to minister.

● Follow the guidance of the Holy Spirit as He leads you into obedience to Christ.

● Remain alert to the responses of other Christians.

These guidelines, along with other elements of recognition and discovery, should help those who are earnestly wishing to find their niche in the service and work of God.

DEVELOPING SPIRITUAL GIFTS

Colossians 4:17; 1 Timothy 4:12-16; 6:20-21; 2 Timothy 1:6-14; 4:1-5; James 5:15.

The above listed scriptures show the attitude of Paul and James toward the development of gifts. It must not be thought that the Holy Spirit is inadequate in His ability to give a perfect and complete gift to the several believers to use. His endowments are totally complete and absolute, but it is the human channel for their use as well as receptivity which is involved. A gift may very well be perfect in its supply and issue, but quite human in its expression and communication, although the Holy Spirit has promised to help our infirmities. The promise of God through Paul is not abrogated or minimized, that "God is able to make all grace abound toward you, so that in all things at all times, having all that you need, you will abound unto every good work. You will be made rich in every way so that you can be generous on every occasion, and through us your generosity will result in thanksgiving to God" (2 Corinthians 9:8, 11, NIV).

The discovery and recognition of spiritual gifts does not mean that nothing on the human side is to be done in their development. It is never out of order to study, to cultivate, to nurture, and to stimulate a possession, or an endowment for its most efficient use. We are workers together with the Holy Spirit, and He will not do for us what we can do for ourselves. He will do for us and others only what we cannot possibly do ourselves.

The Scriptures imply that we are to be dedicated instruments of His glad service.[5] This will lead us to cultivate and develop whatever gifts we have. *The existence of a gift is a call to its exercise and full use.*[6] Faithfulness in the utilization of a gift enriches its serviceability to others. Again, this is no reflection upon the Spirit, but upon the human vessel.

When one Christian uses his gifts to the glory of God, encouragement flows to others — they are edified. All are mutually enriched.[7] This is why Paul wanted to visit Rome. Gifts may thus be sharpened by their exercise in the community of faith. It is a never-ending process of mutual inspiration.

It may also be possible that through the faithful exercise of one gift the Holy Spirit may communicate another gift. Or it may simply be discovered and recognized by the one who has been faithful. This seems to have been the experience of Philip as cited above in Acts 8. The exercise of his gifts of showing mercy and of wisdom may have led to the discovery and use of the gift of evangelism.

One of the obvious results of recognizing one's gift or gifts is the fact that gladness is brought to both the edified believers and the one through whom the Spirit has been pleased to give the edification. For this reason, a person who delights to do the will of God will be most likely the acting, participating bearer of fruit in every sense of the meaning of that term.

SUMMARY

While God bestows His gifts as He sees best for the advancement of His kingdom, it is possible for us to have some knowledge of what they are. We may then work with the Holy Spirit in the development and exercise of them. However, that knowledge will probably be given in due course as in seeking God's will we gladly do whatever tasks for Him come to hand. We should not become so engrossed in trying to discover what our gift or gifts may be that we thwart their usefulness. As we enter open doors, we shall discover God's enabling gifts.

In seeking to know what the will of the Lord is and the work for which we are divinely gifted, we may well consider the services we enjoy doing and the things which seem to be in line with natural abilities. So often God's spiritual gifts complement natural capacities.

In discovering our gifts we need also to take

into account the observation and evaluations of spiritually discerning believers with and under whom we work. Giving attention to the kind of assignment which comes our way from leaders may be a clue. Again, how do we feel within our own spirits? What kind of tasks for the Lord can we do with a feeling of ease and fulfillment?

As we discover our place and gifts, it is important that we take every opportunity to improve that gift or gifts. We are responsible to enlarge and enhance them through study, prayer, and exercise. This all may lead to ever-widening ministry in the evidence of God and the church.

What Do You Think About These?

1. Give at least three principles or guidelines which are helpful in discovering one's gifts.

2. Which gifts are you personally attracted toward?

If You Want to Dig a Little Deeper

Write in your own words what you understand is meant by developing one's spiritual gifts.

Bible References Relating to This Chapter

[1] Timothy 4:12-16; 6:20-21; 2 Timothy 1:6-14
[2] Colossians 4:17
[3] 1 Corinthians 12:31; 4:1; 1 Timothy 3:1
[4] 1 Corinthians 12:11; Hebrews 2:4
[5] Romans 12:6-8
[6] 1 Timothy 4:14
[7] Romans 1:11

FRUIT AND GIFTS ASSURE CHARACTER AND SERVICE

13

Relevant Scriptures: 1 Corinthians 13:1-13;
John 15:1-8; Psalm 1:1-3

Fruit has to do with character. Gifts have to do with serving. Fruit is permanent. Gifts will cease. To be fruitful, then, is better than to be gifted. Jesus suggests as much. He declared that it is by bearing fruit that we show ourselves to be His disciples.[1] He did not say that the Christian's unique identification would be their gifts.

But to bear good fruit is not good enough. Goodness must manifest itself in loving service for others.[2] Being is to result in doing. Accordingly, God makes provision that we may both be and do. By His grace through Christ, ministered to us by the Holy Spirit, we may be saved from our sinning and have our hearts made clean. Through the same Spirit He bestows enabling gifts for effective service in His kingdom.

The epitome of all the Spirit's fruit is love — God's kind of love. Luther referred to it as "the living essence of the divine nature which beams full of goodness." It has been declared also to be "the greatest thing in the world."

The Apostle Paul gave a definitive description of what God's love is and does in our lives. What he wrote appears in our New Testament as 1 Corinthians 13. The very fact that a man like Paul wrote such a passage is in itself a convincing illustration of how God transforms men's lives and fills them with himself. The mind from which those inspired words came was once full of bitterness and anger. The hand which penned them was once stained with human blood. But no more!

He tells us that love supersedes eloquence, is greater than the ability to prophesy, greater than being able to unravel all mysteries and to understand all things. Love is even better than faith, he says. Faith is but the channel by which God's love comes to us.

Let us see what he says this most noble fruit actually is. Henry Drummond, writing of Paul and of 1 Corinthians 13:4-7, is helpful when he says that love is a compound thing and illustrates it like this:

"It is like light. As you have seen a man of science take a beam of light and pass it through a crystal prism, as you have seen it come out on the other side of the prism broken up into its component colors — red, blue, yellow, violet, orange, and all the colors of the rainbow — so Paul passes this thing, love, through the magnificent prism of his inspired intellect, and it comes out on the other side broken up into its elements.

"In these few words we have what one might call the spectrum of love, the analysis of love. Will you observe what its elements are? Will you notice that they have common names; that they are virtues which we hear about every day; that they are things which can be practiced by every man in every place in life; and how, by multitude of small things and ordinary virtues, the supreme thing . . . is made up."[3]

THE ELEMENTS OF LOVE

The elements in Paul's spectrum of love are actually a listing of those qualities which combine to make the Christian the kind of person he is. They show what Christian behavior is to be like.

The Christian is to be *patient*. The emphasis here is upon patience in relationship with other persons rather than in dealing with situations generally. "It takes greater love to be long-suffering with people than with circumstances. . . . The demonstration of love in the midst of a clash of personalities may well prove to be love's acid test."[4]

The Christian is to be *kind,* that is to be gentle, considerate, sympathetic, helpful. Kindness is the everyday practice of our faith in relation to anyone in need whom we are in a position to help. It was one of Jesus' most conspicuous characteristics. To remind himself of this, Sir Wilfred Grenfell, the eminent missionary doctor of Labrador, used to keep a plaque on the wall of his surgery where he could see it readily amid the harassing pressures from the long lines of boorish but needy patients who thronged him daily. It read:

> "He did things so kindly,
> It seemed His heart's delight
> To make poor people happy
> From morning until night."

Christians are to be *generous* toward others and *humble*. In competition with other persons they are not to envy, to make a display of themselves, or to boast. To desire the possessions and advantages which others have or to begrudge others having them, to feel the need to be conspicuous and to call attention to one's accomplishments: these tendencies often spring out of a sense of insecurity or perhaps from an undue regard for material goods and position, or maybe from an unwholesome self-image. But to experience God's love brings an awareness of security, a satisfying assurance and contentment. It helps put values in better perspective. It enables us to heed Paul's admonition: "Do not think of yourself more highly than you ought, but rather think of yourself with sober judgment, in accordance with the measure of faith

God has given you" (Romans 12:3, NIV).

An aging minister may have had this passage in mind as he was talking with a man of means who had just remarked, "I do not need to ask the Lord for anything; if I want something I go out and get it." "You might ask the Lord for humility," chided the man of God.

Love prompts Christians to be *courteous*. It is never rude, ill-mannered, or offensive. The follower of Christ may not know all of the rules in the etiquette book, but he will always seek to be polite, for politeness, after all, is but the art of showing by external signs the internal regard we have for others. A selfish person cannot be genuinely courteous, and a truly Christian one will not be discourteous.

Politeness can of course be superficial, but we must not become so involved with "big issues" that we forget the small, common courtesies. If we are not nice to people, they may well get the impression that we don't really love them. Courtesy always has witnessing value.

The fruit of love is *unselfish*. It does not insist upon its rights, in having its own way. The person who has God's love in his heart is much more concerned about what he owes life than what life owes him. He lives to give not to get. No one can be happy who lives for himself. True joy comes in losing oneself in a cause that is bigger, better, more worthy, and more enduring than himself. Self-forgetfulness marked Jesus' every step from Bethlehem to Calvary. We who follow Him must expect to walk that same path.

Another element in love's spectrum is *good temper*. Love is good-natured. Irritability, exasperation, a touchy, difficult disposition, a resentful attitude: all of these are out of place among Christians. Wesley remarked that the person who possesses God's love "is not provoked to sharpness or unkindness toward anyone. Outward provocations indeed will frequently occur, but he triumphs over all." God's love will enable us to overcome any of the real or fancied aggravations which come to us.

Love is utterly without guile, absolutely *sincere*. It is open, frank, transparent. How refreshing to meet and be with people like that! Deception, cover-up, duplicity, falsehood are the order of the day. But Christians are to be different. They are not to be pressed into this world's mold.

HOW TO BEAR SPIRITUAL FRUIT

Viewing its beam through the prism of God's Word we see that love is not simply "a thing of enthusiastic emotion. Rather, it is a strong expression of the whole round Christian character — the Christlike nature in its fullest development."

How may we be sure that that kind of love and all of the other fruit of the Spirit is increasingly present in our lives? Jesus answered this question for His apostles during the last hours He was with them. He illustrated His lesson with references to the vine and the branches. The account is recorded in John 15:1-8. He declared, "I am the vine; you are the branches. If any man remains in me and I in him, he will bear much fruit; apart from me you can do nothing" (v. 5, NIV).

Jesus in this way tells us that He is the source of spiritual life, the beginning. We as branches are the channels of that divine life. As the life-giving sap in the vine flows from the roots and body of the vine to every branch, so it is that we, the branches, draw our life from Christ.

The primary purpose of the branch is not simply to draw upon the source of life. It is rather to bear fruit. Only then does it accomplish its purpose. So, while we as Christians are to draw on the eternal resources of divine life as found in Christ, we are to bear fruit that will be winsomely evident to those about us. With that fruit we are to help meet the hunger and need in the lives of men all around us.

Just as truly as the natural branch is wholly dependent upon the vine by whose sap it is sustained, so *there can be no true Christian life and fruitbearing apart from an intimate relationship with Christ.* No amount of presumptive effort apart from Him will bring genuine results for the kingdom. According to Marcus Dodd's translation, Jesus says that without Him "ye cannot do anything which is glorifying to God, anything which can be called fruitbearing."

To become a branch in the vine requires a definite act of God. The Apostle Paul refers to this as being grafted into the vine.[5] This process is carried out only as we choose to have it performed. Different from the vine's branch which has no power to choose whether or not it is a part of the vine or whether it shall remain so, in the spiritual realm we may offer ourselves for the grafting.

As we turn from sin in repentance and trust Christ for salvation, we are grafted into Him through the power of the Holy Spirit. That is an essential and truly memorable occasion. But that is not the end. Having been grafted in, we must remain. We have been brought into a new relationship with God through conversion, and that relationship must be maintained.

For the persons who abide in Christ, fruit appears in their lives naturally, just as grapes appear on the vine. And not only so. Just as the vine bears its grapes in season, so the Christian bears fruit in season. This is emphasized even more by the psalmist's tree, planted by the water (Psalm 1:3).

For the Christian to bear fruit in season means that in the midst of conflict, hatred, and bitterness, he bears only love. In the hour of long waiting and tension the one who abides in

Christ bears patience. In the face of injury and ridicule the Christian is gentle and kind. Among those who are shady in their speech and conduct, even among the vile, he is unquestionably clean and good. When things seem to be "going to pieces" he has faith and hope. When no one seems to notice as he labors obscurely to do his task, he is faithful and dependable. When things are in an upheaval and chaos seems to prevail, he has poise, he keeps his head, he knows where he stands. When success comes, pride does not sweep him off his feet. He is humble. Nor is he overwhelmed when demoted. His life is not loose and careless, but is disciplined and controlled. He is not haphazard. He consistently directs himself toward worthwhile, well-chosen goals.

Every branch of the vine bears these fruits in some measure. But there is always room for greater productivity. In order to obtain this greater amount of fruit, the husbandman often prunes or cleanses the branch that it may be more productive. We shall never get beyond the need for pruning, but we are taught in the Word that through sanctification of the spirit, through the infilling of the Holy Spirit, we are cleansed from the carnal propensities of the human heart. In conversion we are cleansed in that we live clean lives. In sanctification we are cleansed inwardly, our motives are purified. Fruitbearing becomes more abundant. Peter spoke of this benefit of sanctification when he recounted the experience of Cornelius and his household. Peter declared: "God . . . put no difference between us and them, purifying their hearts by faith." Without this cleansing, fruitbearing will always be limited.

Fruitbearing also means that there is ever present a willingness for and capacity for Christian service. James, the Lord's brother, speaks of this when he says that true religion and undefiled before God also includes works. It means to serve our generation as we have opportunity. We are to do such menial things as visiting the fatherless and widows in their affliction.[6] We are to reach all men, however we may, with the benefits of the gospel.

Service cannot take the place of character nor can character take the place of service. Both must grow together.

SUMMARY

In all valid Christian experience and life there is a balance between being and doing — between character and serving. To emphasize one above the other is an error.

The Bible leaves no question regarding the kind of person the Christian is to be. He is to be like Christ, because he does in fact draw his spiritual life from the Lord. To bear the fruit of love is as natural for the believer as it is for the vine to bear grapes, because it is from Christ that his life comes.

Nor does the Bible leave any question regarding the kind of service Christians are to render. They are to serve effectively, lovingly, and self-forgetfully, as did their Lord.

That kind of fruitbearing and serving are possible only because the Holy Spirit, God himself, is present and at work in and among us.

What Do You Think About These?

1. Why must character and good deeds go together in Christian living?

2. What are the nine characteristics of the Christian considered in this session?

3. How does one go about obtaining these qualities in his life?

4. How can one be assured he will have the spiritual gifts necessary for effective Christian service?

5. What are some other characteristics of the Christian?

If You Want to Dig a Little Deeper

List nine elements of love cited in this chapter. Illustrate each by incidents in the lives of New Testament persons, and by incidents in the lives of present-day Christians you have encountered.

Bible References Relating to This Chapter
[1]John 15:8
[2]Matthew 20:26-28
[5]Romans 11:17-24
[6]James 1:27

Bibliography
[3]Henry Drummond, *The Greatest Thing in the World.*
[4]J. C. McPheeters, "The Epistle to the Corinthians" *Proclaiming the New Testament.*